CROSSROADS OF MORTALITY

CROSSROADS OF MORTALITY

A Pastoral Journey of Comfort and Hope

MARY PAMELA EKE

Foreword by Eric Hillabrant

WIPF & STOCK · Eugene, Oregon

CROSSROADS OF MORTALITY
A Pastoral Journey of Comfort and Hope

Wipf & Stock
An Imprint of Wipf and Stock Publishers
199 W. 8th Ave., Suite 3
Eugene, OR 97401

www.wipfandstock.com

PAPERBACK ISBN: 979-8-3852-7183-2
HARDCOVER ISBN: 979-8-3852-7184-9
EBOOK ISBN: 979-8-3852-7185-6

VERSION NUMBER 03/11/26

To my mom, Louisa Eke of blessed memory; to those who have stood at the edge of life's great unknown with courage, with grief, with wonder; to the caregivers, companions, and silent witnesses who walk alongside others in their final seasons; and to every soul who has asked what it means to live while facing the mystery of death.

Crossroads of Mortality is dedicated to you.

Contents

Foreword by Eric Hillabrant ix
Preface xi
Acknowledgments xv
List of Abbreviations xvii

PART I | FACING THE CROSSROADS

1 Dust and Eternity 3
(The Theology of Mortality)

2 Fragile Yet Full of Glory 22
(Grief and the Human Conditions)

3 Living Towards the End 45
(Spiritual Readiness and Inner Peace)

4 Between Faith and Medicine 65
(Navigating End-of-Life Dilemmas)

5 Naming the Silence 83
(The Language of Suffering, Mystery, and Presence)

PART II | AT THE CROSSROADS

6 When Love Stays 101
(Caring for the Living Amid Dying)

7 The Companioned Path 116
(Grief Care in Christian Ministry)

8 Self-Care and Mental Hygiene 136
(Care for Oneself Leads to Better Care for Others)

PART III | HOPE BEYOND THE HORIZON

9 Where Death Meets Resurrection 149
(The Hope That Holds Us)

10 Death, Not an End 161
(A Final Word of Courage and Grace)

Appendix 1 167
Prayers and Scriptural Readings for End-of-Life Care

Appendix 2 171
Reflective and Discussion Questions

Bibliography 175

Index 181

Foreword

Crossroads of Mortality offers a thoughtful and theologically grounded exploration of pastoral care at the end of life. Reading this work reaffirmed the significance of ministry with the dying and the bereaved that has shaped my own professional and spiritual life. As a chaplain and director of the pastoral care department at Endeavor Health Swedish Hospital in Chicago (formerly Swedish Covenant Hospital), I have found that accompanying patients and their loved ones through serious illness, dying, and grief represents some of the most demanding and meaningful work undertaken in healthcare settings. Sr. Dr. Mary Pamela Eke's book reflects this complexity with clarity, depth, and pastoral sensitivity.

The pastoral competencies that characterize Sr. Pamela's ministry at Swedish Hospital are evident throughout the text. As a chaplain, she engages with the practical challenges faced by patients, families, and healthcare professionals while remaining attentive to their emotional and spiritual needs. Her work with grieving families is marked by both compassion and clarity, providing steady support in moments of profound loss. Equally noteworthy is her engagement with hospital staff, whom she supports through attentive listening and encouragement amid the sustained pressures of clinical work. Drawing on her pastoral skills and encounters, Sr. Pamela's work examines the multifaceted realities of caring for those who are dying, those who grieve, and those who provide care within emotionally and ethically charged environments. Her work is a careful consideration of the role of faith in human responses to mortality, how individuals interpret suffering, experience finitude, and seek meaning in the face of loss.

As her colleague in chaplaincy, I believe that Sr. Pamela is exploring some of the most important questions people in ministry face. How do we help those who are unprepared for the reality of death process its impact in the compressed time and fierce emotions following the shock of a terminal diagnosis or a sudden and unrecoverable health crisis? Her book is a resource for caregivers that adds depth to their personal psychosocial and theological knowledge. It is also a source for practical skills that integrate theoretical knowledge into the work of ministry. The narrative dimension of the book enhances its value as a work of practical theology. Sr. Pamela's use of storytelling invites reflection, allowing readers from clinical and nonclinical settings to consider how the theoretical insights in her work might enhance their own pastoral understanding and practice.

This volume will be of value to readers across a range of contexts, including theological education, parish ministry, and healthcare chaplaincy. I have found its insights helpful in reflecting on and refining my own pastoral practice. Ultimately, *Crossroads of Mortality* does not promise mastery over death or grief; rather, it situates ministry within a posture of humility and dependence. In doing so, Sr. Pamela reminds readers that pastoral care in the face of suffering bears witness not to human control, but to the enduring and mysterious love of God that sustains both caregivers and those they serve.

Rev. Eric R. Hillabrant, MDiv, BCC
Chaplain and Director of Pastoral Care
Endeavor Health Swedish Hospital
Chicago, Illinois

Preface

Death is a universal reality, yet it remains one of the most profound and challenging aspects of human experience. Whether sudden or expected, the finality of death often stirs deep questions about meaning, faith, love, and loss. For individuals, families, and communities, the journey through dying and grieving is both intensely personal and deeply communal, demanding courage, wisdom, and compassion. As caregivers, whether pastors, chaplains, family members, or friends, or even the medical team, our role is to walk alongside those facing this sacred threshold, offering comfort and hope amid uncertainty and sorrow.

This book—*Crossroads of Mortality: A Pastoral Journey of Comfort and Hope*—is a journey shaped by the experiences, voices, silences, and stories of many individuals across Chicago and beyond. While some of these stories are true life experiences, using pseudonymous names for the individuals involved, others are just fictions told by the author to aid readers' understanding.

It seeks to provide guidance and encouragement for those tasked with this sacred duty, those who are overwhelmed with the experience of grief, and even to those who want to be conscious of the fact that there is a time for everything (Eccl 3:1), and everyone has got a date on the calendar. It offers practical tools, theological reflections, and compassionate insights for navigating the complex realities of mortality. It serves as a resource for those who minister to the dying, those who support grieving families, and those who seek to reflect on their own spiritual journey through life's fragility and finite nature.

This book is divided into three parts, each addressing a vital stage of the journey at the crossroads.

PART I—FACING THE CROSSROADS

At the heart of life's journey lies an inevitable confrontation with mortality. "Facing the Crossroads" (Part I) offers theological, emotional, and spiritual guidance for individuals and communities navigating the complexities of death and dying. Beginning with chapter 1, "Dust and Eternity," this section explores the theological foundations of mortality across various religious traditions and presents a pastoral reflection on the role of hope and resurrection. Chapter 2, "Fragile Yet Full of Glory," addresses grief as a profound human condition, outlining the stages of grief, its psychological impacts, and the diverse cultural responses to death. Chapter 3, "Living Towards the End," calls readers into inner reflection, guiding them toward spiritual readiness, forgiveness, and embracing mortality with peace. The tension between faith and medical interventions comes into focus in chapter 4, "Between Faith and Medicine," where end-of-life dilemmas and ethical decisions are discussed with spiritual sensitivity. Finally, chapter 5, "Naming the Silence," reflects the language of suffering, the power of silence, and the mystery surrounding death, offering tools for accompanying those in their final moments when words can no longer suffice. Together, these chapters invite readers to face mortality not as an enemy, but as a sacred threshold illuminated by hope and faith.

PART II—AT THE CROSSROADS

While death itself draws near, the spiritual work of supporting the living continues. "At the Crossroads" (Part II) focuses on the ministry of presence, grief care, and practical rituals of farewell. In chapter 6, "When Love Stays," attention is given to the emotional and spiritual needs of families walking alongside the dying, offering practices that foster connection and healing. Chapter 7, "The Companioned Path," delves deeper into the spiritual and psychological aspects of grief care, recognizing the complexity of mourning and the need for ongoing support beyond the moment of death. This chapter also addresses complicated grief, resilience, and the hope that can emerge from profound loss. Turning the lens inward, chapter 8, "Self-Care and Mental Hygiene," emphasizes the essential practice of caregiver wellbeing, reminding those in ministry and care roles that tending to their own physical, emotional, and spiritual needs is not optional but foundational to serving others effectively. In this part, readers are encouraged to accompany others through death, even as they care for their own hearts along the way.

PART III—HOPE BEYOND LIMIT

At the culmination of the pastoral journey stands the enduring promise of hope. "Hope Beyond Limit" (Part III) centers on the theological and spiritual affirmation that death is not the end. Chapter 9, "Where Death Meets Resurrection," offers a profound reflection on hope in the face of death, emphasizing the Christian promise of resurrection as both anchor and comfort amid grief. This hope is not abstract but becomes a lived reality in faith practices, communal worship, and the stories of those who find strength through trust in God's presence even in their final hours. In chapter 10, "Death, Not an End," the book closes with words of courage and grace, affirming life's sacred journey and the mystery of passing into eternity. Songs, prayers, and reflective stories in this chapter seek to leave readers not in sorrow but in hopeful expectation of the life to come. Through this final part, readers are invited to embrace mortality with the assurance that death leads not to despair, but to transformation and renewal in God's enduring love.

At the heart of this book is the belief that even in death, God's presence abides. As Ps 23: 4 (NIV) says: "Even though I walk through the darkest valley, I will fear no evil, for you are with me; your rod and your staff, they comfort me." Also, Rom 8:38–39 (NIV) says: "For I am convinced that neither death nor life, neither angels nor demons, neither the present nor the future, nor any powers, neither height nor depth, nor anything else in all creation, will be able to separate us from the love of God that is in Christ Jesus our Lord." In the moments of deepest sorrow and loss, the promise of divine love and the hope of resurrection provide strength and solace. This conviction does not erase the pain of death but transforms it.

Throughout the journey, the enduring message remains clear: at every crossroads, there are the enduring relationships, legacies, and hope that persist beyond life. By embracing the complexities of mortality with honesty and faith, we can find ways to honor both the sanctity of life and the sacredness of death. This book invites us to step into this journey with open hearts, prepared to offer comfort and to bear witness to the power of love and hope that transcends even death itself.

May this work serve as a guide and companion, and equip those in service with the tools to minister effectively and offer inspiration as they walk alongside others through the valley of the shadow of death. Together, let us seek to embody the light of God's love in the darkest moments and to proclaim the eternal hope found in Him (Ps 23:4).

With grace and hope,
Mary Pamela Eke

Acknowledgments

FIRST, AND FOREMOST, I am grateful to God Almighty who made all things possible. May His name be praised now and forever. Amen! I am extending my heartfelt gratitude to the patients, families, and caregivers who, knowingly or unknowingly, shared moments of profound humanity. Your courage in the face of the unknown became the quiet heartbeat of this book.

To my colleagues in the Pastoral Care Department, the interdisciplinary team, and to all staff at Endeavor Health Swedish Hospital in Chicago, thank you for your ministries to our patients and families, for your support and companionship in the often-unspoken corners of life and death, and for being inspirational to this work. Having you as colleagues and friends, I learnt how to listen deeply and speak gently.

To my family (religious and biological) and friends, your support and affection kept me going during the long study and writing sessions, and I owe you a debt of gratitude. You reminded me that reflection requires rest, and that storytelling is sacred. Your efforts were instrumental in the realization of this work and I thank you immensely.

I cannot forget to express my deepest gratitude to all of my endorsers. Thank you for your invaluable support, trust, and confidence in my work. Your advocacy has not only validated my efforts, but has also provided the crucial momentum needed to bring this writing to fruition. The time and talent you invested into this work cannot be forgotten.

To my editor and publishing team, thank you for your insight, your patience, and your belief in the importance of these pages. You helped shape not only the manuscript, but the message within it.

Finally, to those who have died and left echoes in these pages, your lives mattered. May these words honor the thresholds you crossed.

List of Abbreviations

APA	American Psychological Association
ALS	Amyotrophic Lateral Sclerosis
CBT	Cognitive Behavioral Therapy
CGT	Complicated Grief Treatment
DNR	Do Not Resuscitate
EMDR	Eye Movement Desensitization and Reprocessing
EOL	End of Life
ESV	English Standard Version
ICU	Intensive Care Unit
MBSR	Mindfulness-Based Stress Reduction
NIV	New International Version
PET	Prolonged Exposure Therapy

PART I

Facing the Crossroads

1

Dust and Eternity

(The Theology of Mortality)

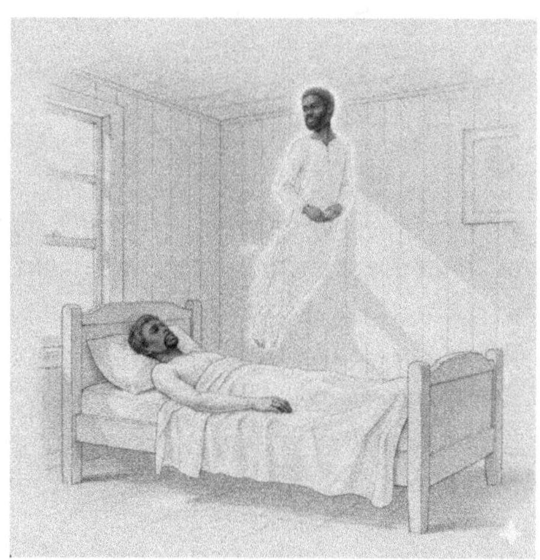

STORY: THE GARDEN AND THE GARDENER

In a quiet village, there lived an old gardener named Ken. His hands were weathered, his eyes gentle, and his heart full of prayers. He tended the village garden, not for money, but for love. For fifty years, he had grown roses that climbed like praises, wheat that bowed like prayer, and olive trees that stood like old saints.

Ken was beloved, but he was also fading. Age clung to him like nightfall.

On a beautiful morning, a boy named Samuel found Ken sitting beneath a tree, eyes closed, face to the sky. The boy sat beside him.

"Are you dying, Ken?" Samuel asked, not out of fear, but wonder.

Ken opened his eyes and smiled. "'Dying' is a word we use for a door, Samuel. And doors are for passing through."

"Where does the door lead?"

"To the other garden," Ken said. "The one the Master prepared."

"Will it be like this one?" Samuel asked.

Ken shook his head gently. "This one is only a whisper. That one is the song."

Samuel sat in silence. Then, hesitantly: "Are you afraid?"

Ken looked toward the skyline where light melted into gold. "No. Christ passed through the door first. And He left it open."

"But we'll miss you."

"And I will miss you. But love is not undone by death. It is fulfilled by it."

Samuel frowned. "I don't understand."

Ken reached into the earth and plucked a seed. "This seed must fall into the soil and die before it becomes a tree. That is the way of God. We mourn the seed, but rejoice in the tree."

Then he placed the seed in Samuel's hand. "Remember this when I'm gone."

That season, Ken passed, and in the other season, Samuel planted the seed, and years later, a tall tree grew in the garden. Children played beneath it, and Samuel, now grown, told them the story of the man who wasn't afraid to die, because he believed in a Savior who turned graves into gardens.

Reflection: *Christian theology teaches that mortality is not the end but a transformation. Death, though painful, is not a tragedy when seen through the eyes of Christ, it is a passage into fullness of life, where sorrow is swallowed up in glory.*

THE IRREVOCABLE END OF a creature's life-sustaining functions is called death. On the calendar, everyone has got an irreversible date and time when death would occur. It's a known fact, and a necessary end, yet takes humanity unaware and unprepared. It happens biologically when critical systems, such as the heart, brain, and lungs, fail and are unable to heal. On another level, death involves the breakdown of metabolic activity and the degradation of cells, leading to decomposition. Kübler-Ross, in her work *On Death and Dying*, describes death as a transformative process, often seen in religious contexts as a gateway to another existence. She went on to say that "in many spiritual traditions, death is regarded not as an end but as a beginning, a passage to another realm of existence where the soul continues its journey."[1] While the specific markers of death, such as brain death or cardiac arrest, vary slightly across medical and legal definitions, it universally signifies the end of an organism's ability to sustain itself.

Death has deep philosophical importance that extends beyond the biological domain. Many people view it as the end of personal identity and consciousness, which begs the question of what life is all about and whether there is such a thing as an afterlife. According to Margulis and Sagan, "Death, biologically speaking, is the irreversible cessation of the organism's systemic functions. It is the moment when cells cease to metabolize, and the organism can no longer sustain itself."[2] Some philosophical perspectives hold that death is a natural part of life and that by highlighting the fleeting nature of human experiences, they give them meaning. Others view it as a mystery that defies explanation and prompts contemplation on what, if anything, happens after death.

Culturally and spiritually, death is deeply intertwined with human belief systems and practices. Many traditions frame death as a transition rather than an end, with concepts like reincarnation, spiritual liberation, or afterlife shaping rituals and worldviews. In *Islam*, for instance, death is a passage to the afterlife, souls are judged by Allah on the day of judgment, and their eternal fate is determined based on their deeds. "Islam sees death as the moment when the soul leaves the body, beginning its journey toward judgment. The ultimate resurrection will reunite body and soul, determining eternal reward or punishment."[3] *Judaism* views death as a natural part of life, with varied beliefs about the afterlife. Some traditions emphasize resurrection, while others focus on spiritual continuity. Gillman asserts that "Judaism offers diverse perspectives on death, from the concept of bodily resurrection in Messianic times to the belief in the immortality of the soul. These reflect the central hope in God's justice and mercy."[4] *Hinduism and Buddhism* focus on liberation from the cycle of samsara (rebirth) known as birth, death, and rebirth. In their thought, "death is not the end but a phase in the perpetual cycle of samsara, governed by karma. The atman (soul)

1. Kübler-Ross, *On Death and Dying*, 67.
2. Margulis and Sagan, *What Is Life?*, 12.
3. Nasr, *Heart of Islam*, 122.
4. Gillman, *Death of Death*, 145.

continues its journey, reincarnating in various forms until it achieves moksha, the liberation from material existence."[5] *Many Indigenous traditions* see death as a transition to a spirit world, where ancestors play a significant role in guiding the living. To them, "death is not the end but a transformation. The deceased continue to exist as spirits, maintaining a connection with the living and the natural world."[6]

In summary:

- **Hinduism and Buddhism** focus on liberation from the cycle of rebirth.
- **Christianity and Islam** emphasize resurrection and eternal life.
- **Judaism** offers varied views on the afterlife, including resurrection and immortality.
- **Indigenous traditions** often perceive death as a transition to the spirit world.

These diverse traditions highlight cultural and theological understandings of death, each reflecting unique paths to addressing its mystery and significance. These interpretations influence how societies cope with loss, commemorate the deceased, and make sense of mortality. Whether approached scientifically, philosophically, or spiritually, death is a universal incidence that shapes the human experience in profound and complex ways.

In the Christian tradition, death is interpreted as a profound spiritual and physical reality, rooted in the narrative of creation, fall, and redemption. According to Scripture, death entered the world through sin, as described in Gen 3:17–19. Adam and Eve's disobedience disrupted their perfect communion with God, introducing both physical mortality and spiritual alienation (Rom 5:12). In this view, death is not merely a biological end but a consequence of humanity's estrangement from the Creator, affecting both body and soul.

The transformative power of Jesus Christ's death and resurrection redefines the Christian understanding of death. By bearing the penalty of sin, Christ's sacrifice restores the relationship between humanity and God, and His resurrection demonstrates victory over death (1 Cor 15:54–57). For Christians, this means that death is not an end but a gateway to eternal life. The apostle Paul expresses this hope, describing death as a gain for believers

5. Flood, *Introduction to Hinduism*, 86.

6. Harvey, *Animism*, 78.

who will be united with Christ (Phil 1:21). This perspective permeates the experience of mortality with profound hope and assurance.

Furthermore, the doctrine of resurrection assures Christians of their future bodily transformation and eternal life in God's presence. Revelation 21:4 portrays a vision of the ultimate triumph over death, where sorrow and suffering are eradicated. According to Wright, "The Christian eschatological promise encompasses the resurrection of the body, the renewal of creation, and the final triumph of God's justice and mercy. It offers a vision of eternal life, where all creation is reconciled and restored under God's reign."[7] This eschatological promise shapes Christian attitudes toward life and death, encouraging a faith-filled response to mortality. It also inspires pastoral care to emphasize compassion and hope, providing solace to the grieving and affirming the sanctity of life in all its stages.

THE ORIGIN OF DEATH

The origin of death is a concept that has been explored across various cultures and religious traditions, often linked to the idea of sin, disobedience, or a fundamental flaw in existence. In many belief systems, death is seen as a transition or consequence that follows a disruption in the natural order of life. In the biblical narrative, God created humanity to live in perfect harmony with Him, with the potential for eternal life. However, when Adam and Eve were placed in the garden of Eden, they were given one command: not to eat from the tree of the knowledge of good and evil (Gen 2:17). When they chose to disregard God's command and ate from the forbidden tree, they introduced sin into the world. As a result, the perfect relationship they once shared with God was broken, and death became the inevitable consequence of their disobedience.

In Gen 3:17–19, God pronounces the consequences of this disobedience, stating that the ground would be cursed, and Adam would toil for his sustenance. The most profound consequence, however, was the introduction of physical death. God told Adam, "For dust you are and to dust you will return" (Gen 3:19). This declaration marked the end of humanity's potential for eternal life in the garden of Eden and introduced mortality as a central part of the human experience. Death, which was once foreign to creation, became an inescapable reality for all humanity, as it entered the world through sin.

7. Wright, *Resurrection*, 219.

Philosophically, death can be viewed as an inherent and unavoidable aspect of the life cycle, as well as a normal component of the human experience. According to several traditions, death results from the constraints of the physical universe, the frailty of the human situation, and the imperfections of existence. In this way, death is not always a punishment but rather a necessary component of the life cycle, which consists of birth, development, aging, and death. According to this perspective, death is a normal occurrence, even if it frequently has profound emotional, existential, and spiritual meaning for both people and civilizations.

Theologically, Rom 5:12 explains that sin and death spread to all people through the actions of Adam. As it states, "sin entered the world through one man, and death through sin." This passage indicates that death is a direct result of humanity's rebellion against God. The concept of death as a result of sin is not merely physical but also spiritual, as humanity's disobedience led to separation from the Creator. This separation is seen as the spiritual death that now accompanies all people, as they are born into a fallen world. However, the Christian faith holds that through Jesus Christ's death and resurrection, this separation can be healed, offering the hope of eternal life in God's presence once again.

DEATH AND REDEMPTION

Looking at death and redemption from the Christian perspective, they are foundational concepts rooted in the life, death, and resurrection of Jesus Christ. Christianity teaches that all humans are born into sin and separated from God, but through the sacrificial death of Christ on the cross, redemption becomes possible (1 Cor 15:54–57). Jesus' death, viewed as the ultimate act of love and sacrifice, paid the price for humanity's sins, offering believers the chance for forgiveness and eternal life. Redemption, in this context, is not merely a pardon but a transformation, a spiritual rebirth where individuals are reconciled with God and empowered to live according to His will. The resurrection of Christ symbolizes victory over death, not just physically, but also spiritually, offering hope that death is not the end, but a passage to eternal life with God for those who accept Christ's gift of salvation. The apostle Paul emphasizes this transformed understanding of death as "gain" for those who are in Christ (Phil 1:21).

On the social perspective, death and redemption can be seen as a reflection of the collective struggles and healing within a society. Just as individuals face personal sin and transformation, communities, nations, and cultures also experience moments of profound loss, conflict, and injustice. Redemption, in this context, involves the process of reconciliation, healing, and rebuilding after suffering or wrongdoings. It can manifest in efforts to right past wrongs, seek justice, and restore harmony. For example, after periods of social or political turmoil, a society may go through a process of collective redemption, acknowledging its faults, forgiving transgressions, and striving to build a better future. The idea of social redemption is especially powerful in post-conflict situations where people work to overcome division and restore unity.

In both the Christian and social realms, redemption requires more than just acknowledgment of wrongdoing; it demands action, change, and a commitment to something greater. Christians believe that redemption comes through God's grace, transforming the individual's heart and mind to live in alignment with His teachings. Social redemption, similarly, involves individuals coming together to heal from the wounds of the past and create a more just, compassionate, and peaceful future. Ultimately, both perspectives emphasize the transformative power of grace, forgiveness, and reconciliation, whether it's between individuals and God or between members of a community striving for collective healing and progress.

THE RESURRECTION AND THE AFTERLIFE

The resurrection is a central doctrine in many religious traditions, particularly in Christianity, where it holds profound significance. In Christianity, the resurrection refers to the belief that Jesus Christ rose from the dead on the third day after His crucifixion. This event is seen not only as a confirmation of His divine nature but also as a promise of eternal life for all believers. (1 Thess 4:14). The resurrection is a symbol of hope and victory over sin and death. For Christians, Jesus' resurrection is the guarantee that death does not have the final word, and those who follow Him will be raised to eternal life in the presence of God. The resurrection is celebrated annually during Easter, marking the triumph of life over death and the possibility of personal transformation.

Christians

In Christian theology, the afterlife is intrinsically linked to the resurrection. Christians believe that after death, the soul continues to exist and is judged by God. The resurrection signifies a future bodily return to life for the righteous, who will be granted eternal life in heaven, free from pain and suffering. Those who are not reconciled with God through faith in Jesus Christ are believed to face eternal separation from God, commonly referred to as hell. The afterlife, therefore, is viewed as the ultimate destination where individuals experience the eternal consequences of their choices in this life. The resurrection promises a physical transformation where believers receive glorified bodies, free from the imperfections of earthly existence, to live forever with God in heaven (Rev 21:1–4).

Thus, Christian eschatology envisions death as a transition to an eternal state. The faithful are promised a share in God's eternal kingdom, where pain, suffering, and death are no more (Rev 21:4). This vision provides a profound sense of purpose and direction, encouraging individuals to live in a manner that reflects their hope in the life to come. This theory challenges caregivers to examine a person's spirituality in terms of transcendence, growth, relational characteristics, values/beliefs, and meaning.[8]

Islam

Beyond Christianity, many other religions also feature beliefs in resurrection and an afterlife, though the details vary significantly. In Islam, for example, the resurrection is a key principle, where every individual will be resurrected for judgment by Allah. Qutb, in his work *In the Shade of the Qur'an*, describes the resurrection as a fundamental event that signifies the reuniting of the body and soul. According to Qutb, this event is central to the Islamic understanding of the afterlife and divine justice. He writes: "The resurrection is the point where all actions are accounted for, and the body is rejoined with the soul. It is a day of reckoning, where the just are rewarded and the unjust face punishment. The resurrection demonstrates Allah's absolute control over life and death and is an essential component of the Islamic view of the afterlife."[9] Muslims believe that the righteous will be rewarded with eternal life in paradise, while the wicked will be punished in hell.

8. Lydon-Lam, *Models of Spirituality*, 18.
9. Qutb, *In the Shade of the Qur'an*, 468.

Jewish

Judaism holds diverse views on resurrection and the afterlife, shaped by historical and theological developments. Traditional Jewish belief, particularly in Orthodox Judaism, affirms a future bodily resurrection of the dead, especially during the messianic age. This belief is rooted in biblical texts such as Dan 12:2, which speaks of many who "sleep in the dust" awakening to eternal life or disgrace, and is elaborated upon in rabbinic literature like the Talmud. The concept of *olam ha-ba* (the world to come) is central to Jewish eschatology, referring both to a posthumous spiritual realm and a future redeemed world. Rabbinic Judaism generally upholds resurrection as a core principle of faith, as reflected in Maimonides' Thirteen Principles. In contrast, Reformed and other liberal Jewish movements often interpret the afterlife metaphorically, focusing more on spiritual continuity or moral legacy than on physical resurrection.[10]

Jehovah's Witnesses

Jehovah's Witnesses hold a distinctive view of resurrection and the afterlife, centered on their interpretation of the Bible. They believe that death is a state of nonexistence, with no conscious afterlife. However, they maintain a strong belief in a future resurrection. Jehovah's Witnesses teach that after Armageddon, God will resurrect the righteous and many of the unrighteous to life on a restored earthly paradise. This hope is based on Scriptures such as John 5:28–29 and Acts 24:15. Unlike traditional Christian views of an immortal soul, Jehovah's Witnesses reject the idea of a soul living on after death, emphasizing instead a physical resurrection granted by God's memory and power. Only a limited group of 144,000 anointed individuals, they believe, will be resurrected to heavenly life to rule with Christ, while the majority will live forever on earth.[11]

Hinduism and Buddhism

Hinduism and Buddhism, on the other hand, do not focus on bodily resurrection but instead emphasize the cycle of reincarnation, where souls are

10. Jacobs, *Jewish Religion*, 417.

11. Watch Tower Bible and Tract Society of Pennsylvania, *What Does the Bible Really Teach?*, 73–75.

reborn into new lives based on the karma accumulated in previous ones. Doniger, in her book *The Hindus: An Alternative History*, contrasts Hindu beliefs about death and the afterlife with the concept of resurrection. She writes: "Hinduism's approach to life after death is fundamentally different from the linear notion of resurrection. Here, the soul transmigrates through various forms, determined by its actions and desires. The idea of physical resurrection is absent, as the focus lies on liberation from the corporeal existence through spiritual growth."[12] In these traditions, the ultimate goal is not merely resurrection but liberation from the cycle of rebirth, reaching moksha (in Hinduism) or nirvana (in Buddhism), where the soul is freed from suffering and the cycle of reincarnation (birth, death, and rebirth).

Liberation from this cycle (nirvana—which marks the end of the cycle, rather than a physical or spiritual resurrection) is the ultimate spiritual goal. Here are scholarly interpretations of Buddhist perspectives on life after death, touching upon themes that might conceptually parallel resurrection. According to Keown, "Buddhism teaches that there is no permanent self or soul to be resurrected. Instead, what continues after death is a stream of consciousness propelled by karma. This stream eventually ceases when nirvana, the cessation of suffering and the cycle of rebirth, is achieved."[13] Harvey, in turn, emphasizes that "while resurrection implies a reconstitution of the same individual, Buddhism emphasizes that rebirth involves a continuity of karmic effects without a permanent self. The cycle of rebirth is marked by impermanence and suffering, and the ultimate aim is to escape this cycle by attaining nirvana."[14] These interpretations show that Buddhism views life after death in terms of rebirth, where continuity exists not as a resurrection of an individual self, but as a process governed by cause and effect until liberation is achieved.

Summarily, the resurrection and the afterlife continue to evoke deep philosophical and existential questions, especially regarding the nature of existence, morality, and ultimate purpose. For many, the concept of resurrection provides comfort and assurance, offering a sense that life has meaning beyond its temporary struggles. It suggests that suffering and death are not the end but part of a larger divine plan that leads to a greater, eternal reality. In a more secular or existential context, the idea of an afterlife can provoke questions about legacy, the nature of consciousness, and the possibility of

12. Doniger, *Hindus*, 214.

13. Keown, *Buddhism*, 47.

14. Harvey, *Introduction to Buddhism*, 34.

immortality through memory or spiritual continuity. Ultimately, whether viewed through the lens of religion or philosophy, there are implications to how one lives his or her life. Therefore, there is need for individuals to reflect on the nature of life, death, and what may await beyond this world.

PRACTICAL IMPLICATIONS

Understanding man's mortal nature has profound practical implications, influencing both individual and societal perspectives on life, purpose, and ethical decision-making. On a personal level, acknowledging mortality encourages individuals to live with greater intentionality, prioritizing meaningful relationships, personal growth, and the pursuit of fulfillment. It fosters a sense of urgency to make the most of limited time, leading to wiser choices about health, career, and personal aspirations. Furthermore, awareness of mortality can inspire people to cultivate virtues like humility, gratitude, and compassion, as they recognize the finite nature of life and the shared human experience of impermanence.

On a broader societal level, recognizing human mortality shapes cultural, religious, and philosophical perspectives, influencing legal, medical, and ethical systems. For instance, end-of-life care, funeral traditions, and legal frameworks around wills and inheritance are all shaped by the awareness that life is transient. Additionally, mortality awareness plays a crucial role in public health initiatives, encouraging preventive care and responsible decision-making regarding life-threatening risks. Philosophically, it challenges societies to find meaning beyond material achievements, fostering values that emphasize community wellbeing, legacy, and intergenerational responsibility. Ultimately, an understanding of mortality prompts both individuals and societies to create a life of purpose, responsibility, and ethical consciousness. The following subheadings are essential in understanding and addressing the practical implications of mortality.

Personal Implications

At an individual level, mortality profoundly influences how people live their lives. The awareness of death often motivates individuals to prioritize meaningful relationships, pursue goals, and engage in self-reflection. Many people adopt practices such as journaling, meditation, or creating legacy projects to grapple with their mortality. Additionally, mortality awareness prompts practical actions such as drafting wills, creating advanced directives, and making end-of-life care plans. These preparations alleviate burdens on loved ones and ensure one's wishes are respected. Mortality also influences health behaviors. For instance, individuals may adopt healthier lifestyles to extend their lifespan or enhance the quality of their remaining years. The conscious recognition of death can also evoke existential anxiety, prompting people to seek solace in religion, spirituality, or community engagement to find meaning and purpose.

Family and Community Implications

On a familial level, mortality necessitates preparedness for the emotional, logistical, and financial challenges that arise when a loved one passes away. Families often face the task of navigating grief, which Garten et al. say is "the normal reaction to a significant loss,"[15] arranging funerals, and managing properties. Practical considerations like life insurance, savings, and inheritance planning can significantly reduce stress during these times.

In communities, mortality fosters rituals and traditions that honor the dead and provide collective solace. For example, cultural ceremonies such as funerals, wakes, or memorial services serve dual purposes: they allow individuals to process grief while reinforcing community bonds. Community organizations, including religious institutions and support groups, often play critical roles in providing pastoral care and counseling services.

Societal and Institutional Implications

Mortality influences public policy, legal structures, and healthcare systems in society. An essential component of the healthcare system is end-of-life care, which includes hospice and palliative treatments. Investments in education, materials, and moral standards that honor patient autonomy and cultural diversity are necessary to guarantee access to these services. It propels improvements in public health programs and medical research. Society's dedication to life preservation is demonstrated by initiatives to lower premature mortality through immunization programs, disease prevention campaigns, and better access to healthcare.

15. Garten et al., *Palliative Care and Grief Counseling*, 6.

Environmental and Global Implications

Mortality has an impact on environmental policies, resource distribution, and population dynamics worldwide. International aid systems are strained and inequality is made worse by high death rates in some areas, which are frequently brought on by poverty, illness, or violence. Coordinated international action is needed to address these gaps, such as enhancing access to healthcare and halting climate change, which disproportionately impacts vulnerable groups. Furthermore, as people look to leave a sustainable legacy for future generations, mortality awareness fuels environmental conservation efforts. This viewpoint, which emphasizes the need of protecting ecosystems and resources for the continuation of human life, is consistent with the idea of intergenerational equity.

Summarily, the practical implications of mortality extend far beyond the individual, influencing families, communities, and global systems. By addressing these implications thoughtfully, society can mitigate the challenges associated with death while honoring its inevitable role in the human experience. Preparing for mortality, through personal actions, social support systems, and institutional frameworks, not only eases the burden on individuals and families but also fosters resilience and compassion in the face of life's most profound certainty.

BIBLICAL PERSPECTIVES ON DUST AND ETERNITY

Biblical perspectives on dust and eternal life is a temporary phase of human existence, marked by the fragility and impermanence of life. The human condition is shaped by the reality of physical death, which serves as a reminder of humanity's limitations and dependence on God. In biblical thought, death is not merely an end but a transition, reflecting the consequences of sin and the fallen state of the world. However, mortality also carries a purpose, urging people to seek wisdom, live righteously, and prepare for what lies beyond this life. Through faith, believers find meaning in their transient existence, knowing that earthly life is not the ultimate reality.

Eternal life, as presented in the Bible, is not just endless existence but a restored and perfected relationship with God. It is portrayed as a gift rather than an entitlement, granted to those who embrace faith and align their lives with divine principles. This eternal state is often contrasted with the suffering and decay of the present world, offering hope beyond the constraints of mortality. Biblical teachings emphasize that eternal life is not only a future promise but also a present reality, as believers experience spiritual renewal and communion with God even while on earth. This perspective shifts the focus from mere survival to purposeful living, anchored in the expectation of divine fulfillment.

The tension between mortality and eternal life shapes the Christian worldview, encouraging a life of faith, hope, and moral responsibility. Rather than fearing death, believers are called to view it as a passage to something greater, where justice, peace, and divine presence are fully realized. This belief in eternity influences ethical choices, personal priorities, and attitudes toward suffering and loss. While mortality is a universal human experience, biblical teachings affirm that it is not the final word: eternal life offers a promise of restoration, joy, and unbroken fellowship with God.

The following subthemes are derived throughout Scripture, offering both comfort and direction to humanity.

Mortality: A Universal Reality

The Bible identifies mortality as an inevitable aspect of human existence, rooted in the story of humanity's fall. In Gen 2:16–17 (NIV), God warns Adam and Eve that disobedience will lead to death: "For when you eat of it you will certainly die." Their eventual sin (Gen 3) results in the introduction of death into the world, both physically and spiritually. Mortality becomes a consequence of separation from God, highlighting humanity's dependence on Him for life.

Scripture frequently reflects on the transient nature of human life. Psalm 103:15–16 compares life to grass that flourishes briefly before withering: "The life of mortals is like grass; they flourish like a flower of the field; the wind blows over it and it is gone, and its place remembers it no more." Similarly, Jas 4:14 (NIV) describes life as a "mist that appears for a little while and then vanishes." These passages remind Christians to approach life with humility, recognizing its fleeting nature. Despite its brevity, mortality serves a purpose in God's design. Psalm 90:12 teaches, "Teach us to number our days, that we may gain a heart of wisdom." Awareness of life's limitations encourages individuals to prioritize what truly matters and to seek a deeper relationship with God.

The Promise of Eternal Life

While mortality is an unavoidable reality, the Bible also proclaims the promise of eternal life through faith in Jesus Christ. John 3:16 (NIV), one of the most well-known verses, summarizes this hope: "For God so loved the world that he gave his one and only Son, that whoever believes in him shall not perish but have eternal life." This promise offers a profound contrast to the finality of physical death.

The resurrection of Jesus Christ is central to the Christian understanding of eternal life. First Corinthians 15:54–57 (NIV) celebrates this victory: "'Death has been swallowed up in victory.' . . . Thanks be to God! He gives us the victory through our Lord Jesus Christ." Through His resurrection, Jesus not only defeats death but also provides humanity with the assurance of their own resurrection and eternal future. Revelation 21:4 (NIV) offers a vision of the fulfillment of eternal life, where God will "wipe every tear from their eyes. There will be no more death or mourning or crying or pain, for the old order of things has passed away." This imagery conveys the ultimate hope of a restored creation where humanity dwells eternally with God.

Implications for Daily Life

The Bible's teaching on mortality and eternal life has profound implications for how Christians live. First, it provides hope and comfort in the face of life's challenges and the inevitability of death. First Thessalonians 4:13–18 (NIV) reassures Christians that death is not the end, but a transition to eternal life with Christ. This assurance enables individuals to face mortality with peace and confidence. Hence, the promise of eternal life calls us to live with moral accountability. Second Peter 3:11–12 (NIV) urges Christians to "live holy and godly lives" in anticipation of Christ's return. Awareness of eternity encourages a focus on spiritual growth and the pursuit of righteousness.

Summarily, the hope of eternal life motivates Christians to share their faith. Jesus' Great Commission in Matt 28:19–20 calls His followers to make disciples of all nations, spreading the message of salvation. This mission reflects the urgency of helping others discover the gift of eternal life. Though mortality serves as a reminder of life's brevity and the consequences of sin, the promise of eternal life offers hope and a future secured through Christ's resurrection.

THE ROLE OF HOPE AND RESURRECTION IN PASTORAL THEOLOGY

Pastoral theology, as a branch of Christian theology, focuses on the practical aspects of ministry, offering guidance and care for individuals within the Christian faith community. Central to pastoral theology is the role of hope and resurrection, two interwoven themes that speak profoundly to the human experience of suffering, loss, and redemption. According to Volf, the resurrection signifies the triumph over sin, death, and despair, offering individuals the assurance of eternal life and divine restoration.[16] This theological hope allows pastors to guide individuals through times of grief or existential crisis, offering a framework in which suffering is viewed not as the end but as part of a larger narrative that culminates in God's victory. Pastoral care, thus, becomes a practice that not only comforts but also strengthens individuals by connecting them to this hope, providing both a present and future sense of peace and purpose.

On the other hand, the resurrection of Jesus, while an eschatological event, has profound implications for the lives of believers in the here and now. In Tennent's opinion, the resurrection is not merely an abstract theological concept but a transformative force that empowers individuals to live in a way that reflects the values of the kingdom of God.[17] This transformative aspect is key: resurrection is seen as a dynamic reality that enables believers to live new lives, empowered by the Holy Spirit. Pastoral care providers, therefore, are called to help individuals understand that the resurrection invites them into a life of moral renewal and spiritual transformation, where the old self is put to death and a new life is embraced. This notion aligns with the idea that Christian hope is not just a future expectation but also a present reality that shapes the individual's daily life, empowering people to live in accordance with the resurrection's transformative power.

Furthermore, the resurrection plays a pivotal role in offering hope amid the challenges and suffering of life. As Ward suggests, the resurrection functions as the foundation for a Christian's enduring hope, even in the face of personal and collective suffering. Pastoral theology, in this

16. Volf, *Exclusion and Embrace*, 132.

17. Tennent, *Invitation to World Missions*, 189.

regard, focuses on helping individuals contextualize their pain within the larger narrative of God's redemption plan. By grounding their ministry in the promise of resurrection, pastors offer a vision of restoration and hope, reminding individuals that suffering is temporary and that God's ultimate victory over death and evil will be fully realized in the future.[18] The resurrection, then, becomes a source of both emotional and spiritual resilience, motivating believers to persist in faith and trust in God's redemptive work. Through this lens, pastors can offer not only comfort but also a compelling vision of the future that empowers individuals to face life's trials with hope.

Hope

Hope is a cornerstone of the Christian faith and an essential element in pastoral theology. It is through hope that individuals are able to endure hardship, face uncertainty, and live with a sense of purpose and expectation. In the context of pastoral care, hope is not a mere optimistic outlook but a deep, theological conviction rooted in God's promises and faithfulness. It is the hope of redemption, restoration, and ultimate victory over evil and suffering that fuels the Christian's journey.

Pastoral theology teaches that hope is both an individual and communal experience. On a personal level, pastors provide hope to individuals who are grappling with loss, illness, or despair. This is done through counseling, prayer, Scripture, and the reminder that suffering is not the final word. Hope becomes an anchor, a source of strength that helps individuals endure present struggles while looking forward to future transformation. Thus, humanity is reminded that life is not defined by one's suffering or failures, but by God's unshakeable love and the promise of a renewed life.

Communally, hope is embodied in the church as a body of believers, fostering communal hope, particularly in times of crisis. Whether addressing social injustices, natural disasters, or collective grief, individuals and congregations are called to remain steadfast in the face of adversity, encouraged to bear one another's burdens and to find strength in the collective witness of the church. By nurturing a hopeful community, people are provided with a space where they can experience the collective power of faith and hope, reinforcing the belief that God is always present and working through the body of Christ.

18. Ward, *Christian Ethics*, 104.

Hope also empowers individuals to transcend the limitations of their present circumstances. It fosters resilience, enabling people to move forward even when the future seems uncertain. For instance, during times of loss, grief, or failure, individuals are offered the strength to keep going, knowing that God is present in their suffering and that there is a greater purpose that can emerge from even the most challenging situations.

The Resurrection

The resurrection of Jesus Christ is the ultimate expression of hope in Christian theology, and its significance cannot be overstated. The resurrection signifies victory over sin, death, and the forces of evil, offering believers a tangible hope for the present and future. Pastorally, the resurrection is not only a historical event but also a present reality that shapes the life of the believer. It is the foundation of Christian hope, demonstrating that life is stronger than death, light is greater than darkness, and good ultimately prevails over evil. In providing care, individuals are helped to understand that the resurrection is not merely an abstract doctrine but an event that directly impacts the lives of persons. Through the resurrection, Christians are given the assurance of eternal life, the forgiveness of sins, and the hope of transformation. The role of the caregiver often involves walking with individuals through their own personal "resurrections," moments of spiritual renewal, healing from trauma, and the rebirth of faith in the midst of doubt and despair.

In practical terms, the resurrection reminds individuals that death, in all its forms, is not the end. Pastors who bear the message of resurrection can offer comfort and assurance to grieving families, knowing that death does not have the final say. Through funeral services and memorials, pastors emphasize the Christian belief that death is not a permanent separation but a transition to eternal life with God. This belief helps individuals face mortality with peace, knowing that their loved ones, through the resurrection, are in God's presence. Just as Jesus was resurrected, individuals can experience spiritual and emotional restoration. Therefore, whether dealing with addiction, depression, or relational conflict, the resurrection provides a profound hope that God is always working to restore and heal.

Finally, hope and resurrection are foundational to pastoral theology, guiding the work of pastors as they seek to bring comfort, healing, and transformation to individuals and communities. The resurrection of

Jesus Christ, the ultimate expression of hope, serves as both a theological foundation and a source of practical hope in pastoral ministry. Through the lens of hope and resurrection, individuals are helped to navigate life's trials, find healing in the midst of grief, and live with the assurance of eternal life. These theological themes, deeply embedded in Christian tradition, are essential and remain vital in the ministry of care, compassion, and transformation.

2

Fragile Yet Full of Glory

(Grief and the Human Conditions)

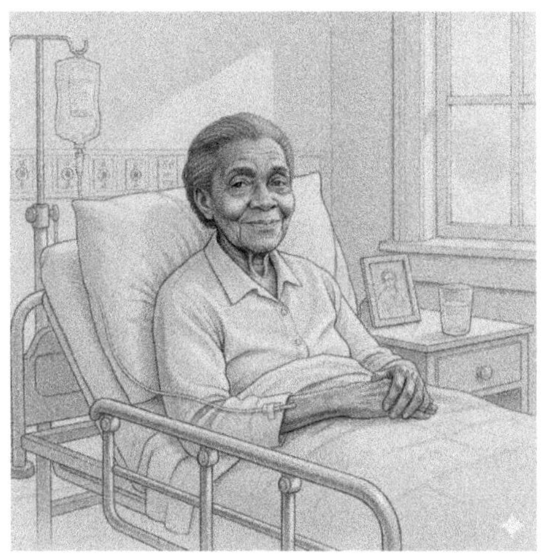

STORY: LET THE LIGHT SHINE

There lived an old lady, Pam, and her daughter at the seaside. Often, they lit their lamps for the fishermen and others to see during the night. Pam had lived there for many years with her daughter, Mary. They shared everything, laughter echoing through the stone halls, stories whispered while storms howled outside. Mother and child were best friends and loved each other.

One rainy period, the sea grew cruel. A fierce illness came upon Pam, and though Mary tried everything, warm blankets, healing herbs, quiet prayers, the light in her mother's eyes dimmed, and one cold morning, she was gone.

Mary kept the light burning. Every night, she lit the flame. But inside, her own light flickered. The sea that once sang to her now roared with sorrow. She would stare out into the waves, asking, "Why must we love, only to lose? Why are we born if we must leave?"

One night, in her grief, Mary forgot to light the lamp. The darkness stretched across the river like a shadow of her sorrow. That night, a fisherman nearly lost his way, narrowly steering his boat to safety.

In compassion, Mary promised to never forget to let the light shine for others to see. As she ponders, she heard her mother's voice in her heart:

"We must keep the light shining, child. Not to stop the storm. Not to calm the sea. But to gleam, even in grief, so others can find their way."

Tears streamed down Mary's face. It didn't end the ache. But something shifted. Her grief became a part of the light, not a darkness to hide, but a warmth to share. She began telling her mother's stories again. Singing her songs. And every evening, she lit the lamp, in love, in memory, in pain, and in hope.

Reflection: *The human experience of mortality and grief is like putting up the light in the middle of a storm. We lose what we love, and the loss leaves us hollow. But grief is also a sign of the love we carry, and in time, that love can become light again, helping others through their darkness. We don't move on from loss; we carry it forward and make it part of what helps us live.*

Regardless of culture, religion, or personal preferences, death is an inevitable aspect of the human experience. Despite the fact that everyone experiences death, there are notable variations in how people view and respond to it. Grief is the emotional response to loss and is as diverse as humanity itself. It is impacted by a person's psychological composition, relationship with the departed, societal conventions, and personal beliefs. The experience of death and mourning is extremely complicated and individualized due to the complex interplay of these components.

The natural emotional reaction to death, especially the loss of a loved one, is grief. Kübler-Ross, a pioneer in the study of death and grief, explored the human experience of mortality and grief in her groundbreaking work *On Death and Dying*. In order to better understand how people deal with the reality of death and loss, she developed the five stages of grief: denial, anger, bargaining, depression, and acceptance. According to Kübler-Ross, people may alternate between stages in a very individualized manner.[1] Different scholars have also explored the human experience of mortality and grief from various perspectives, including psychological, neurological, and philosophical angles. Recent research suggests that grief is a fundamental emotional response necessary for human survival, with nonadaptive forms leading to severe psychological conditions such as major depressive disorder.[2]

Philosophically, grief is seen as an essential process of adjusting to loss. It involves reconciling conflicting thought patterns and gradually restructuring one's sense of self and reality after a significant loss. Unlike purely psychological accounts, grief is viewed as a necessary adaptation to the social and cognitive structure of human life.[3] Cultural variations in grief expression are also significant. Studies indicate that mourning rituals, intensity, and duration of grief differ widely across cultures, shaping individuals' experiences and coping mechanisms.[4] In some cultures, such as in many parts of Africa and the Middle East, public displays of grief are encouraged and seen as a necessary part of the mourning process. In contrast, Western cultures often emphasize stoicism, with an expectation to "move on" quickly. Rituals, such as funerals, memorial services, and commemorative acts, serve as communal outlets for grief and provide a sense of closure.

In Kübler-Ross' later work, *On Grief and Grieving* (coauthored with David Kessler in 2005), they expanded on the emotional and psychological aspects of loss, stressing that grief is a unique journey influenced by personal, cultural, and spiritual factors. Kübler-Ross and Kessler also acknowledged the importance of finding meaning in loss and how resilience can emerge from the grieving process.[5] However, modern perspectives reveal that there is no particular way to grieve, and individuals may move through these stages in unique and unpredictable ways.

1. Kübler-Ross, *On Death and Dying*, xx.
2. Castro-Figueroa, "Biopsychosocial Approach to Grief," 110.
3. Hilberdink et al., "Bereavement Issues," 1.
4. Ratcliffe et al., "On the Appropriateness of Grief," 2.
5. Kübler-Ross and Kessler, *On Grief and Grieving*, xxx.

THE FIVE STAGES OF GRIEF

1. **Denial**: In this initial stage, individuals struggle to accept the reality of their loss. Denial serves as a psychological defense mechanism to buffer the shock and pain. People may believe there has been a mistake or feel emotionally numb. Kübler-Ross describes denial as a temporary response that allows the individual to slowly absorb and process the grief at their own pace.[6] For care providers, gently acknowledging the reality of the loss while providing a safe space for individuals to express their disbelief can help them move forward.

2. **Anger**: Once reality begins to set in, individuals often experience anger. This anger may be directed at themselves, others, medical professionals, or even the deceased. It stems from feelings of helplessness and injustice. Kübler-Ross emphasizes that anger is a natural and necessary stage, as it helps people begin to externalize their pain and engage with their emotions.[7] Care providers can validate these emotions, helping individuals express them constructively rather than suppress them.

3. **Bargaining**: In this stage, individuals attempt to regain control or change the situation by making deals or promises, often with a higher power. They may think, "*If only I had done something differently, maybe this wouldn't have happened.*" Bargaining is characterized by "what-if" and "if-only" statements, reflecting a desire to reverse or prevent the loss.[8] For those experiencing loss, this stage can feel isolating, and care providers can assist by exploring these thoughts without judgment, guiding the care receiver toward acceptance of the unchangeable.

4. **Depression**: As the full impact of the loss becomes evident, individuals experience profound sadness. This stage may involve feelings of emptiness, hopelessness, or withdrawal from daily activities. Kübler-Ross distinguishes between *reactive depression*, which arises from immediate circumstances (e.g., funeral planning, financial worries), and *preparatory depression*, which comes from accepting that life has permanently changed.[9] Chaplains/therapists can support those

6. Kübler-Ross, *On Death and Dying*, xx.
7. Kübler-Ross and David Kessler, *On Grief and Grieving*, xx.
8. Kübler-Ross, *On Death and Dying*, xx.
9. Kübler-Ross and David Kessler, *On Grief and Grieving*, xx.

grieving by normalizing these emotions and encouraging healthy coping mechanisms. For grieving individuals, it is essential to understand that this stage is not a sign of weakness but a natural part of the healing process.

5. **Acceptance**: In the final stage, individuals come to terms with the loss and find ways to move forward. Acceptance does not mean the absence of grief but rather a shift in perspective, and grief becomes integrated into one's life experience. People may begin to find meaning in their loss and adjust to a new reality.[10] Caregivers can help individuals to identify strategies to rebuild their lives while cherishing memories and maintaining meaningful connections to what has been lost.

These stages represent a framework for understanding how individuals cope with loss, particularly in the context of death, though they can also apply to other forms of loss. Beyond Kübler-Ross' model, there are other grief theories like the *Dual Process Model of Coping*, which emphasizes oscillation between processing grief directly and focusing on life's practical adjustments. Accordingly, Worden's *Tasks of Mourning* offer an organized method of dealing with grief, which includes embracing the truth of the loss, overcoming the hurt, acclimating to life without the departed, and keeping in touch with the departed while going on.[11] These tasks emphasize active participation in the grieving process, giving individuals a clear road map for healing. Also, contemporary models, such as the *Continuing Bonds Theory*, highlight that grieving does not necessarily mean letting go of the deceased. Instead, maintaining a healthy, enduring connection through memories, rituals, or symbolic acts can be a source of comfort.[12] Thus, Neimeyer's focus is on finding purpose and reshaping one's identity after loss. He encourages grieving persons to reflect on the significance of their relationship with the deceased and integrating those insights into their life story.[13]

Ultimately, grief is not a one-size-fits-all experience. For those experiencing it, understanding these stages and theories can normalize the range of emotions they may encounter. For care providers, these frameworks provide valuable tools to help clients navigate the difficulties of loss with compassion, patience, and hope.

10. Kübler-Ross, *On Death and Dying*, xx.
11. Worden, *Grief Counseling and Grief Therapy*, 39–45.
12. Klass et al., *Continuing Bonds*, 45.
13. Neimeyer, *Meaning Reconstruction*, xx.

SPIRITUAL AND EMOTIONAL PROCESS OF DYING

The dying progression is deeply intertwined with both spiritual and emotional dimensions. For many individuals nearing the end of life, spiritual questions and concerns may arise, prompting reflections on the meaning of life, one's relationship with God, and the hope for an afterlife. Pastoral caregivers, with their deep understanding of faith traditions and sacred texts, provide a reassuring presence, helping individuals confront these existential questions. By offering prayers, spiritual guidance, and the sacraments, such as the Anointing of the Sick or Holy Communion, pastoral care can help alleviate spiritual distress, ensuring that the dying person experiences a sense of peace and connection with the divine. This spiritual dimension is particularly important, as many individuals seek comfort in their faith during their final days, hoping for forgiveness, reconciliation, and assurance of God's love.

The emotional aspect of dying is equally profound and complex, as individuals face not only their own mortality but also the emotional toll it takes on themselves and their loved ones. Understanding the emotional stages of dying, as explained above (denial, anger, bargaining, depression, and acceptance) can bring comfort to individuals and caregivers can better provide compassionate support in a way that respects each individual's unique emotional journey. Spiritual care providers can listen actively, validate the emotions of the dying person or one's family, and offer a non-judgmental space for expression. This emotional support can significantly reduce feelings of isolation and fear, helping individuals navigate their emotional responses to death. Providing comfort in the form of compassionate listening, reflection, and encouragement can ease anxiety, making the process of dying more bearable.

Pastoral care also addresses the relational aspect of the dying process, facilitating healing and reconciliation between the person who is dying and their loved ones. In many cases, unresolved conflicts, regrets, or feelings of guilt can become prominent at the end of life, heightening emotional distress. Awareness of this fact can guide individuals and their families through processes of forgiveness and expressions of love before it is too late. This can be accomplished through prayer, ritual, or simply encouraging open, honest conversations. For those who have lost relationships due to estrangement or conflict, pastoral care can serve as a mediator, helping to mend broken bonds and foster healing, which can ease the emotional weight of dying.

Lastly, the spiritual and emotional dimensions of dying can be enhanced by the presence of rituals, which provide structure, meaning, and continuity. Rituals like last rites, prayers for peace, or simply holding hands in quiet companionship can offer the dying person a sense of comfort and sacredness. These rituals allow the individual to reflect on their faith, draw closer to their spiritual beliefs, and find solace. For family members and friends, engaging in these rituals alongside the dying person can promote a shared sense of love and unity, providing a collective way to face the inevitable together.

THE PSYCHOLOGICAL IMPACT OF GRIEF

Grief, a natural response to loss, profoundly affects an individual's psychological wellbeing. It is not merely an emotional reaction but a complex process involving cognitive, behavioral, and physical responses. Initially, grief can manifest as shock, disbelief, or numbness, as the mind struggles to process the reality of the loss. This early stage often leads to confusion and difficulty concentrating, as the brain attempts to reconcile the absence of a loved one or significant part of life. Emotional turmoil, such as feelings of sadness, anger, guilt, or even relief, can emerge, reflecting the multifaceted nature of grief and the personal relationship with the loss.

As grief progresses, it can influence one's mental health, sometimes resulting in conditions like depression, anxiety, or prolonged grief disorder. The intense emotions associated with grief may disrupt sleep, appetite, and daily functioning, leading to fatigue and a diminished ability to cope with stress. People may experience intrusive thoughts, such as replaying moments with the deceased or imagining alternate outcomes, which can perpetuate a cycle of distress. Over time, these symptoms may lead to social withdrawal, as individuals struggle to communicate their feelings or fear burdening others. For some, grief can challenge their sense of identity and purpose, particularly if the loss involved a significant role or relationship, such as a spouse or parent.

Despite its challenges, the grieving process also holds the potential for psychological growth and resilience. With support and time, individuals often find ways to integrate their loss into their lives, developing new coping strategies and perspectives. Engaging in meaningful rituals, seeking professional counseling, or participating in support groups can help individuals navigate the complexities of grief. While the pain of loss may never fully dissipate, the psychological impact of grief can eventually lead to a deeper understanding of life, renewed connections, and an enduring appreciation for the relationships and experiences that give life meaning.

HEALTHY COPING MECHANISMS

Healthy coping strategies help individuals process their experiences, regulate their emotions, and maintain a sense of control over their circumstances. Conversely, dysfunctional or nonadaptive coping mechanisms, such as substance abuse or avoidance, may provide temporary relief but often worsen underlying issues, highlighting the importance of cultivating constructive habits. Liese and Beck explained that individuals may turn to substances to escape distressing emotions or psychological pain, gaining temporary relief. However, this reliance on substances tends to exacerbate underlying issues, leading to a cycle of dependency, avoidance, and worsening mental health conditions.[14] They emphasize the importance of addressing core emotional and cognitive patterns while fostering healthier coping strategies to achieve long-term wellbeing.

Coping mechanisms and support systems are essential for navigating the challenges of life, especially during times of stress, loss, or hardship. These mechanisms refer to the strategies individuals use to manage emotional, mental, and physical stress, such as:

- Practicing mindfulness
- Having a support system
- Seeking professional counseling
- Engaging in regular exercise
- Engaging in religious activities
- Expressing emotions through creative outlets

Practicing Mindfulness

Mindfulness encourages presence and acceptance, reducing stress and emotional suffering. It allows individuals to engage with life as it is, rather than dwelling on what was or fearing what's ahead. Through mindful awareness,

14. Liese and Beck, *Cognitive Therapy*, 25–26.

one can experience peace, even amidst pain, and cultivate strength from within. An article by the American Psychological Association (APA) on gratitude and mindfulness explores how mindfulness meditation can help reduce stress and improve emotional wellbeing. It explains the benefits of mindfulness-based stress reduction (MBSR) and how it enhances awareness, resilience, and overall mental health[15] while another article captioned "What Are the Benefits of Mindfulness?" provides a broader perspective on mindfulness, defining it as a moment-to-moment awareness of one's experience without judgment. It highlights the psychological and emotional benefits of mindfulness, including stress reduction and improved focus.[16]

Having a Support System

Support systems play a critical role in reinforcing healthy coping strategies. These systems include family, friends, faith communities, and professional networks that provide emotional and practical assistance during difficult times. Having a reliable support system can foster a sense of belonging and reduce feelings of isolation, helping individuals feel understood and valued. Support systems also serve as a resource for perspective and guidance, as they often include people who have faced similar challenges or are skilled in providing encouragement and advice. Engaging with these systems through conversation, shared activities, or group therapy can create a safe space for expressing emotions and receiving affirmation.

Seeking Professional Counseling

Seeking professional counseling is a valuable coping mechanism for individuals experiencing grief, as it provides a structured and supportive environment to process emotions and develop healthy coping strategies. Grief can manifest in various ways, including sadness, anxiety, guilt, and even physical symptoms, making it essential to seek professional guidance when these feelings become overwhelming. According to Neimeyer et al., grief counseling helps individuals reconstruct their personal narratives, integrate the loss into their lives, and regain a sense of purpose.[17] Counselors

15. American Psychological Association, "Mindfulness Meditation," xx.
16. American Psychological Association, "Mindfulness Meditation," xx
17. Neimeyer et al., *Grief and Bereavement*, 145.

and therapists use evidence-based approaches, such as cognitive behavioral therapy (CBT) and grief counseling, to help individuals navigate their loss and find meaning in their experiences. Research suggests that professional counseling can significantly reduce symptoms of prolonged grief disorder and improve emotional wellbeing.

Engaging in Regular Exercise

Engaging in regular exercise is an effective coping mechanism for individuals experiencing grief, as physical activity has been shown to improve emotional resilience and overall wellbeing. Exercise helps regulate stress hormones, such as cortisol, while increasing the production of endorphins, which enhance mood and reduce feelings of sadness and anxiety. Mura and Carta assert that engaging in regular physical activity can serve as a protective factor against mental health disorders, promoting emotional stability and long-term psychological recovery.[18] Additionally, physical activity provides a structured routine, which can be beneficial in restoring a sense of normalcy after a significant loss. Thus, grieving individuals are encouraged to exercise, because it not only alleviates depressive symptoms associated with grief but also improves cognitive function and sleep quality, both of which are often disrupted during mourning.

Engaging in Religious Activities

Engaging in religious activities serves as a powerful coping mechanism for individuals experiencing grief, providing emotional support, spiritual comfort, and a sense of meaning in the face of loss. Many grieving individuals turn to prayer, meditation, communal worship, or scripture for solace, finding reassurance in their faith and religious community. Religious coping strategies can help individuals reframe their grief within a spiritual context, promoting emotional healing and wellbeing. Religious practices can foster resilience by offering structured rituals such as funerals and memorial services which help individuals process their grief and find closure. Studies suggest that religious involvement is associated with lower levels of depression and anxiety among bereaved individuals, as

18. Mura and Carta, "Physical Activity in Depressed Elderly," 125.

faith-based beliefs often provide a framework for understanding loss and hope for an afterlife.

Expressing Emotions Through Creative Outlets

Expressing emotions through creative outlets is an effective coping mechanism for individuals experiencing grief, allowing them to process their feelings in a constructive and therapeutic manner. Engaging in activities such as writing, painting, music, or dance provides a nonverbal means of communication, helping individuals articulate emotions that may be difficult to express through words. Research suggests that artistic activities can facilitate meaning-making and provide a sense of connection with lost loved ones. Thompson and Neimeyer posit that creative expression helps individuals externalize their grief, reconstruct their personal narratives, and find new ways to integrate their loss into their lives.[19]

For coping mechanisms to be effective, they should align with the individual's personality, cultural background, and circumstances. For example, introverted individuals might find solace in journaling or meditation, while extroverts may benefit more from social activities or group support. Similarly, faith-based support systems can offer spiritual grounding for those who draw strength from their beliefs. Combining personal coping strategies with the strength of a supportive network enables individuals to build resilience, adapt to change, and ultimately grow through life's challenges.

CULTURAL AND SOCIETAL ATTITUDES TOWARD DEATH AND GRIEF

How people and societies react to loss is greatly influenced by cultural perspectives on death and grieving, which have an impact on coping strategies, manifestations of sadness, and rituals of mourning. In some cultures, grief is openly expressed through public ceremonies, wailing, and communal support, while in others, it is regarded as a private and introspective process. Modern globalization and interconnectivity have begun to blur traditional boundaries, allowing for a blending of cultural attitudes toward death and grief. This integration creates opportunities for more inclusive and diverse

19. Thompson and Neimeyer, "Creative Expression and Grief," 395.

approaches, such as incorporating mindfulness and spiritual practices into grief counseling or adopting communal rituals in individualistic settings.

However, cultural and societal attitudes can also create challenges when conflicting cultural attitudes arise, particularly in multicultural families or communities. Recognizing and respecting these diverse perspectives is essential for fostering understanding and supporting individuals through the universal, yet deeply personal, experiences of death and grief. According to Rosenblatt, some of these cultural frameworks not only guide emotional responses but also influence the social support systems available to the grieving.[20] Additionally, religious and spiritual beliefs play a crucial role in shaping one's attitudes and reactions to the emotions, influencing how the individual finds comfort and meaning in loss.

Societal attitudes influence how grief is perceived and accommodated. In some societies, open expressions of grief are encouraged and seen as liberating, while others may stigmatize prolonged mourning or public displays of emotion. These expectations can affect how individuals cope with loss, as societal norms may either validate or suppress their emotional experiences. For example, in collectivist cultures, grief is often a shared experience, with communities gathering to provide support and solidarity. On the other hand, in more individualistic cultures, grievers may feel pressure to "move on" quickly, leading to feelings of isolation or unresolved grief. The societal view of death itself, whether it is seen as a fearful event, a spiritual journey, or a medical failure, also impacts how individuals and families approach end-of-life decisions and rituals.

RITUALS AND SPIRITUAL BELIEFS AFTER DEATH

Rituals and spiritual beliefs play a central role in how individuals and communities navigate life's significant transitions, particularly death and grief. Rituals provide a structured way to honor the deceased, express emotions, and find meaning amid loss. These practices vary widely across cultures and religious traditions but often serve similar purposes: to create a sense of connection with the departed, offer closure, and provide a path toward healing. Whether through funerals, memorial services, prayer gatherings, or symbolic acts like lighting candles or planting trees, rituals offer a tangible framework for processing grief. They also unite communities in shared expressions of love and remembrance, reinforcing bonds of support during difficult times.

20. Rosenblatt, *Grief*, 78.

Spiritual beliefs further shape how people interpret death and approach grief, providing comfort and hope. Many spiritual traditions offer perspectives on the afterlife, reincarnation, or eternal union with the divine, helping individuals find solace in the belief that death is not the end. As earlier stated, in Christian theology, the promise of resurrection and eternal life provides assurance to Christians mourning a loved one, while some other traditions like the Hindus believe in reincarnation. This encourages the understanding of death as a natural part of the soul's journey. These spiritual narratives help individuals make sense of loss, reduce fear of mortality, and inspire hope for eventual reunion or transcendence.

When combined, rituals and spiritual beliefs act as powerful tools for coping and resilience. They provide a sense of continuity and stability, connecting the present moment of grief with a broader narrative of life and meaning. Participation in rituals grounded in spiritual beliefs can offer a sense of purpose and belonging, reminding individuals that they are part of a larger community and cosmic plan. Whether personal or communal, these practices help grievers move through the stages of loss, fostering healing and growth while affirming the enduring significance of their loved ones' lives. Thus, caregivers can support individuals and families by facilitating access to culturally appropriate rituals and respecting their spiritual needs.

CARING FOR THE DECEASED ACROSS RELIGIONS

When a person dies, different religious traditions follow specific rituals and practices to honor the deceased, provide comfort to the family, and ensure a proper transition of the soul. Here is an overview of the next steps in various faiths:

- **Catholicism**: A priest may have administered the last rites (Anointing of the Sick) before the occurrence of the death. After death, prayers are offered for the eternal repose of the soul, and the body can be taken to the morgue, waiting for funeral arrangements to be made. When the family is ready, the body is brought to the Church and the Holy Mass is celebrated, with a prayer of Final Commendation at the end of the Mass. Then the coffin is moved to the cemetery for burial, which is the preferred practice for Catholics, though cremation is allowed but the ashes must be disposed by burial.

- **Protestantism:** Families typically gather for prayer and support. Funeral arrangements, including viewing and a memorial service, are made according to the family's wishes. Cremation and burial are both accepted.
- **Eastern Orthodoxy:** A priest leads prayers immediately after death, and the body is prepared with care. A funeral service, including a procession and prayers for the soul's journey, follows.
- **Islam:** When a person passes, the deceased is immediately washed (*ghusl*) by family members or a designated group of Muslims, wrapped in a simple white shroud (*kafan*), and buried as soon as possible, often within twenty-four hours. Cremation is strictly forbidden. The Janazah (funeral) prayer is performed before burial, with the body placed facing Mecca. (This means that if the body is buried on its right side, the face should be turned toward Mecca. If burial on the right side is not possible, the body may be laid on its back, with the feet pointing toward Mecca and the head slightly tilted to the right. This practice aligns with Islamic teachings that emphasize the importance of facing the Qibla [direction of prayer] both in life [during prayer] and in death. It reflects the belief in resurrection and the soul's journey after death in accordance with Islamic faith.)
- **Judaism:** In Jewish tradition, the body is washed (*taharah*) by a special group (*chevra kadisha*) and wrapped in a simple shroud. Burial occurs quickly, usually within twenty-four hours, as embalming and cremation are discouraged. The mourning period (*shiva*) begins immediately after burial, where family members observe specific grieving customs.
- **Hinduism:** In Hindus tradition, the body of the deceased is treated with respect and cremation is scheduled as soon as possible, usually within 24 hours, because it is believed that the soul (atman) leaves the body and continues its journey according to karma. Shortly after death, family members may recite the name of God or sacred mantras and, if possible, drops of Ganges water are placed into the mouth of the deceased (or when dying). This act is believed to purify the soul and bless its journey onward. If Ganges water is not available, clean water may be used instead, often accompanied by prayers or the chanting of God's name. The body is then washed, dressed in simple (often white) clothing, and laid with the head facing south while prayers are offered. After

that, the chief mourner, who is usually the eldest son, performs the last rites (antyeshti) and lights the funeral pyre, and following cremation the family observes a mourning period of about 10 to 13 days, performing rituals and a final shraddha ceremony to honor the deceased and support the soul's onward journey. Ashes are often scattered in a sacred river to aid the soul's journey toward liberation (moksha).

- **Buddhism:** In Buddhist tradition, when a person dies, the immediate focus is on maintaining a calm and peaceful environment, as a clear state of mind at the moment of death is believed to influence rebirth. Family members often avoid touching or moving the body for several hours—especially in Tibetan Buddhism, where consciousness is thought to remain near the body for some time—while monks or relatives chant scriptures or recite prayers to generate merit and guide the deceased, such as protective suttas in Theravāda traditions or the name of Amitabha in Mahayana practices. Afterward, the body is respectfully washed and prepared for cremation or burial, and funeral rites, along with acts of generosity, are performed to honor the deceased and support a favorable rebirth. These practices reflect core Buddhist beliefs in impermanence, karma, and rebirth.
- **Sikhism:** In Sikhism, when a person dies, the focus is on accepting God's will (hukam) with dignity and remembrance of Waheguru (God). Family members gather to pray, recite verses from the Guru Granth Sahib, and repeat God's name to maintain a calm and faithful atmosphere. The body is washed, dressed in clean clothes (often simple attire), and taken for cremation, usually as soon as reasonably possible. At the cremation, hymns (kirtan) and prayers are recited, and the funeral ceremony, known as Antam Sanskar, honors the soul's journey. Afterward, family and community members may gather at the gurdwara—a Sikh place of worship—for further prayers and readings from the Guru Granth Sahib, emphasizing acceptance of God's will, the soul's return to its Creator, and the importance of living a truthful and devoted life.
- **Indigenous and African Traditions:** Many Indigenous and African cultures have unique rituals that involve community mourning, ancestor veneration, and ceremonial rites. Some traditions emphasize the spiritual transition of the deceased and involve dances, drumming, masquerades, and offerings.

Each religious tradition has specific beliefs regarding the afterlife and how to honor the deceased, reflecting deep spiritual and cultural values.

Summarily, the way society views emotional expression can also affect how long grief is allowed to be felt and how it is exhibited. In some cultures, there is a set period during which grief is expressed publicly, often marked by rituals, mourning attire, or memorial events, after which there is a collective expectation that individuals will return to normal life. In contrast, in more modern or secular contexts, individuals may feel that their grief is expected to be resolved more quickly, without the structured space for emotional processing. As societal expectations shift, there can be tension between individual emotional needs and collective societal norms, complicating the grief experience for many. Recognizing and validating diverse emotional expressions and providing spaces for open dialogue can be key to supporting those who are grieving, allowing for a more compassionate and understanding societal approach to loss.

BRIDGING GAPS WITH COMMUNICATION

Communication is essential for bridging divides during periods of grief and loss, aiding individuals in processing their feelings and creating connections with others. In the process of dying, individuals may experience isolation due to their suffering or ambiguity over the articulation of their intricate emotions. Transparent, sympathetic communication facilitates the exchange of experiences and emotions, alleviating feelings of isolation and allowing individuals to be acknowledged and comprehended. Facilitating candid talk, whether via familial discussions, support groups, or individual chats, enables the bereaved to commence the processing of their grief within a nurturing and caring context. Recognizing loss through conversation affirms the emotional experience, assisting individuals in understanding that they need not confront their sadness in solitude.

Researchers highlight that communication between medical teams and families can be especially difficult during end-of-life care, particularly when a family is in denial over a loved one's imminent death. Effective techniques are essential for managing these challenges while ensuring compassionate care. Bernacki and Block assert that systematic discussions regarding end-of-life care objectives enhance familial comprehension and decision-making. They stress that medical teams should initiate discussions early and provide *consistent*, *clear*, and *compassionate* messaging to prevent misunderstandings and emotional distress.[21]

Facilitating communication is crucial within communities and among diverse ethnic or societal groupings. In certain instances, individuals may find it difficult to articulate their grief due to cultural or societal conventions that inhibit open emotional expression. When disparities in communication arise, it is essential to establish environments where individuals can engage in dialogue that is perceived as secure and respectful of their cultural and personal histories.

This may involve providing alternative forms of expression, such as writing, art, or ritual participation, that allow people to communicate their grief without the need for verbal expression. Acknowledging and respecting these varied forms of communication helps bridge the gap between personal and collective grief experiences, fostering understanding across different backgrounds and communities.

Effective communication can help bridge generational gaps in how grief is experienced and expressed. Younger and older generations often have different ways of understanding and dealing with grief, shaped by changes in societal attitudes, family dynamics, and historical events. Facilitating conversations between generations allows for the exchange of wisdom, coping strategies, and emotional support. For example, older family members may provide valuable advice about traditional grieving rituals, while younger individuals may bring fresh perspectives on seeking professional help or utilizing digital platforms for support. By encouraging intergenerational dialogue, families and communities can strengthen their collective resilience and ensure that the experience of loss is supported by both the past and the present.

Communication Between Family and Care Team

Story: Papa's Care

When seventy-eight-year-old Papa was admitted to the hospital after a fall, his family was in a situation of rapid decisions. Papa had early-stage dementia, diabetes, and limited mobility. His daughter Sarah, who lived nearby, became the primary point of contact with the hospital. His son Ben lived out of state and only got bits and pieces of information through rushed phone calls.

21. Bernacki and Block, "Communication About Serious Illness," 1994–2003.

The first few days were chaotic. Different nurses provided conflicting updates. A social worker mentioned discharge plans before the family had heard a diagnosis. Sarah felt overwhelmed and Ben felt left out. Papa became frustrated, sensing the confusion around him.

Turning Point: A Family-Centered Care Meeting

Sarah requested a care team meeting. The hospital arranged a conference with the primary physician, nurse, physical therapist, and social worker. Sarah and Ben joined; Ben attended via video call. Each team member shared updates and answered questions. The doctor clarified Papa's diagnosis and treatment goals. The therapist discussed what rehab Papa would need. The social worker walked through discharge options.

The care team created a shared communication plan:

Sarah would be the primary family contact.

A weekly update call would be scheduled with both Sarah and Ben.

A summary of care goals and discharge plans was talked about weekly.

Results:

Papa's care became more consistent.

Sarah felt less burdened having clear channels.

Ben felt included and better able to support from afar.

The care team had fewer redundant calls and clearer goals.

When Papa transitioned to a rehab facility, the handoff was smooth; the rehab team already had the family's contact info and a shared understanding of his needs.

Effective communication between families and the medical or care team is essential for ensuring that a patient's time of illness or final days are handled with dignity, respect, and compassion. This process involves clear discussions about medical conditions, treatment options, and the patient's preferences, allowing families to make informed decisions. Healthcare providers are encouraged to use simple, honest, and empathetic language while ensuring that families have the opportunity to ask questions and express concerns. Open conversations help reduce confusion and provide reassurance during a difficult time.

During end-of-life (EOL) care, understanding the patient's wishes is a key part of communication. If the patient is able to participate in discussions, they should be encouraged to express their preferences regarding treatments, palliative care, and life-support interventions. If a patient is unable to communicate, decision-making can be guided by advance directives, living wills, or a designated healthcare proxy. The care team should ensure that these wishes are documented and respected, helping to avoid unnecessary interventions that may not align with the patient's values. A study published in *JAMA* showed that using personalized communication guides helped doctors have more conversations about care goals with patients.[22] The Hospice Foundation of America highlights ethical challenges in dealing with families that struggle to accept a patient's terminal condition. They recommend maintaining patient autonomy, using ethical principles to guide discussions, and addressing family conflicts with a balance of empathy and professional guidance.[23]

Emotional and psychological support for both the patient and their loved ones is vital. Families may experience feelings of grief, fear, guilt, or uncertainty, and healthcare providers should acknowledge these emotions with compassion. Offering access to social workers, chaplains, or grief counselors can help families cope. Encouraging open emotional expression and providing a space for discussions about loss can also ease some of the emotional burden.

Coordination between healthcare providers and caregivers is essential to ensure continuity of care. Whether the patient remains in a hospital, transitions to hospice care, or stays at home, there should be clear communication between doctors, nurses, and family members regarding the care plan. Families should know who to contact for medical support, what to expect in terms of symptom management, and how to handle emergency situations. A well-coordinated approach can reduce stress and improve the patient's comfort.

Cultural and spiritual beliefs play a significant role in how families approach EOL decisions. Healthcare providers should be sensitive to these differences and incorporate spiritual or religious support if requested. The Hospice Foundation of America emphasizes that culturally competent communication and mediation can help align family members' expectations with medical realities.[24] Understanding customs around death and dying helps foster a respectful and inclusive environment. When discussing

22. Curtis et al., "Intervention to Promote Communication," 2028–37.

23. Hospice Foundation of America, "End-of-Life Ethics," xx.

24. Hospice Foundation of America, "Managing Conflict," 29.

difficult topics, using culturally appropriate language and ensuring that families feel heard and understood can make a meaningful difference.

Difficult decisions often arise in EOL care, and families may struggle with choices regarding life support, resuscitation, or stopping certain treatments. If there are disagreements among family members, the medical team can help mediate discussions and offer guidance based on the patient's condition and prognosis. Ballentine, a hospice and palliative care expert, stresses that EOL discussions require healthcare professionals to navigate shifting family dynamics, patient wishes, and emotional responses. She suggests that understanding and addressing these dynamics early can help mitigate conflicts.[25] Providing families with evidence-based recommendations while respecting their perspectives ensures that decisions are made with clarity and compassion.

Finally, support does not end at the moment of death. Families need guidance on what to expect in a loved one's final moments, as well as assistance with practical matters such as funeral arrangements or bereavement resources. Offering grief support and follow-up services can help families process their loss and obtain comfort in knowing that their loved one received dignified and compassionate care.

Some Key Aspects of Effective End-Of-Life (EOL) Communication

1. **Open and Honest Conversations**
    - Encourage open discussions about prognosis, treatment options, and goals of care.
    - Use clear and compassionate language to explain medical conditions, expected outcomes, and available choices.
    - Allow families to ask questions and express their fears, concerns, and expectations.

2. **Understanding Patient Wishes**
    - Discuss advance directives, living wills, and do-not-resuscitate (DNR) orders.
    - Ensure the patient's values and beliefs guide decision-making.

25. Ballentine, *End-of-Life Ethics*, xx.

- If the patient is unable to communicate, involve a healthcare proxy or designated decision-maker.

3. **Emotional and Psychological Support**

   - Acknowledge emotions such as grief, fear, guilt, or uncertainty.
   - Offer support resources, such as social workers, chaplains, or grief counselors.
   - Encourage families to express their feelings and find ways to cope.
   - Encourage time for meaning and closure. Helping families focus on meaningful moments, such as recalling memories, expressing love, and saying goodbye, can shift their perspective from denial to acceptance.[26]

4. **Coordination of Care**

   - Ensure a smooth transition between hospital, hospice, or home care settings.
   - Keep communication channels open between doctors, nurses, palliative care teams, and caregivers.
   - Clarify roles and responsibilities of healthcare providers and family members.

5. **Cultural and Spiritual Sensitivity**

   - Respect cultural, religious, and personal beliefs related to death and dying.
   - Incorporate spiritual care if the patient or family desires.
   - Be mindful of language and customs that may affect EOL decision-making.

6. **Decision-Making and Conflict Resolution**

   - Help families navigate difficult choices about treatments, life support, and palliative care.
   - Mediate conflicts between family members with differing opinions.

26. Hospice Foundation of America, "Managing Conflict," 29.

- Provide evidence-based recommendations while respecting family perspectives.

7. **To Manage Resistance from a Family in Denial**
    - Use a structured communication framework to ensure clarity and consistency.
    - Acknowledge emotions and validate the family's grief while gently reinforcing the medical reality.
    - Engage in shared decision-making by providing families with medical facts while considering their emotional responses.
    - Utilize ethical principles to balance patient autonomy and family concerns.
    - Employ communication tools, such as structured guides, to enhance discussions.

8. **After-Death Support**
    - Guide families on what to expect in the final moments and after death.
    - Offer bereavement resources and grief support.
    - Ensure a compassionate and dignified farewell.

By adopting these strategies, healthcare teams can foster meaningful dialogue, reduce conflict, and provide compassionate EOL care.

John, Maria, Mark, and Others' Experiences

1. **Finding Meaning Through Action:** Following the death of his wife from cancer, John grappled with understanding her loss. To honor his wife's memory, John established a local foundation to promote cancer research and aid families confronting analogous challenges. Ultimately, the endeavor provided him with a sense of purpose and a means to preserve her legacy. He discovered that assisting others in his wife's honor alleviated the pain of her absence, transforming mourning into a catalyst for action. John discovered significance through activity.

2. **Creating a Ritual:** One morning, after the Holy Mass, I observed Maria igniting a candle at the image of Our Blessed Mother. I greeted Maria and conversed with her briefly. Maria, a woman who experienced the sudden loss of her mother, established a monthly tradition of lighting a candle and preparing her mother's favorite dishes. This practice established a bond between Maria and her mother, enabling her family to exchange memories and narratives. Over time, the practice evolved from a painful remembrance into a reassuring tradition.
3. **Seeking Community Support:** Community support after loss is one way of dealing with grief. After the death of his brother in a car accident, Mark joined a local grief support group. Initially hesitant, he found solace in hearing the experiences of others who had also experienced loss. Sharing his story and connecting with people who truly understood his pain made him feel less isolated and offered tools to navigate his emotions.
4. **Focusing on Personal Growth:** Daniel, who lost his father during the COVID-19 pandemic, struggled with feelings of guilt and helplessness. To honor his father's love for learning, Daniel committed to continuing his father's passion for gardening. He transformed his grief into a way to nurture something alive and vibrant, finding healing in the growth and renewal he witnessed.
5. **Leaning on Faith and Spirituality:** When Fatima lost her grandfather, her faith became a cornerstone of her healing process. She turned to prayer and meditation, which helped her feel a sense of connection with her grandfather's spirit and brought her comfort. Her faith community also provided emotional support and helped her find peace in the belief that her grandfather was in a better place.

Each of these stories illustrates the uniqueness of grief and the many ways people adapt to it. These examples also show how channeling pain into action, expression, or connection can help individuals overcome the profound difficulties associated with loss.

Summarily, grief is intrinsic to the human experience, shaping our understanding of life and its finite nature. While the pain of loss is profound, it also underscores the depth of human connection and love. By acknowledging and honoring the diversity of grief, we can better support one another in times of loss, fostering a sense of shared humanity amidst the inevitable reality of mortality.

3

Living Towards the End

(Spiritual Readiness and Inner Peace)

STORY: THE RIVER BEYOND THE BEND

There was once a small village beside a great and winding river. In this village lived an old boat maker named Ikenna, known not only for his skill with wood and water but for the stories he told. He had spent his life building boats for others, yet had never taken the journey downstream, toward the part of the river that disappeared behind a great bend, a place spoken of in hushed tones, called "The Beyond."

As Ikenna grew older, he began carving a boat for himself. It was his finest work, smooth, balanced, and quiet as a whisper on water. Children would ask him, "Where will you go in that boat, Grandpa?" He would smile and point downstream. "To the place where the river bends," he would say, "to see what lies beyond."

Some villagers feared that part of the river. They called it "the end." But Ikenna believed otherwise. "The river doesn't end at the bend," he explained. "It simply disappears from view. Just because we can't see it doesn't mean it stops flowing."

As his time drew near, Ikenna prepared with care. He made peace with old friends, forgave those who had wronged him, and passed on his boat-making secrets to a young apprentice. He spent quiet mornings in prayer, and at dusk, he would sit by the water, watching the current and listening to its song.

One cloudy morning, he placed a lantern at the bow of his boat and gently pushed off from the shore. The villagers stood silently as he drifted downstream, the light glowing steadily until he reached the bend. Then, he was gone.

Some wept. Others wondered. But the young apprentice smiled through his tears. "He's not gone," he said. "He's just gone where we can't see. The river carries on."

Just like Ikenna, each of us is on a journey down a river. Preparing for death from a spiritual perspective means readying our boat, making peace, living with intention, and trusting that what lies beyond the bend is not darkness, but transformation. Death is not the end of the river, only the place where it continues out of sight.

DEATH, AN INEVITABLE PART of the human experience, is often met with a sense of fear, uncertainty, and grief. From a spiritual perspective, however, death is seen not merely as an end but as a transition, an essential passage into a new phase of existence. Different spiritual traditions approach death in unique ways, offering comfort, hope, alleviating pain, and providing guidance for individuals as they prepare for their inevitable departure from this world. Thus, Aydan and Erden posit that "end-of-life care aims to relieve the pain of the individual in the death process and provide a dignified death experience from the moment when the curative treatment no longer brings any benefit."[1] This piece of writing explores the spiritual aspects of preparing for death, highlighting themes of acceptance, meaning, legacy, and the hope for an afterlife that provide solace and a sense of peace during the final stages of life.

Death is a transition to another realm of being, not the end of existence. Numerous religious traditions assert that death is an inherent aspect of life's cycle and warrants no fear. *Christianity*, for example, teaches that death is a gateway to eternal life with God. This belief in the resurrection, life after death, offers profound comfort, especially during times of illness or nearing the end of life. The idea that one's life is part of a greater divine plan, and that death is simply a step in it, allows for a sense of acceptance. For Christians, the resurrection of Jesus serves as a model of victory over death, providing assurance that physical death is not the final chapter but a passage to eternal life.

As it is written, "When the perishable puts on the imperishable, and the mortal puts on immortality, then shall come to pass the saying that is written: 'Death is swallowed up in victory.' 'O death, where is your victory? O death, where is your sting?'" (1 Cor 15:54–55 ESV).

Similar to the Christian faith, the *Islamic tradition* teaches that death is considered a natural transition from worldly life to the afterlife, where individuals will be judged by Allah based on their deeds. It is not the end but a passage to either eternal reward in Jannah (paradise) or punishment in Jahannam (hell). The Quran emphasizes that every soul will taste death (Surah Al-Ankabut 29:57) and that life is a test to determine one's ultimate fate. Islam teaches that the righteous will be granted eternal peace, while those who reject faith will face consequences. The concept of resurrection (Qiyamah) and divine judgment plays a central role, reinforcing accountability and the importance of righteous living.

Accordingly, other spiritual traditions, such as *Hinduism and Buddhism*, view death as part of a continuous cycle of life, death, and rebirth (samsara). In these belief systems, the focus is on the soul's journey rather than the physical end of life. The ultimate goal is to achieve moksha (liberation) or nirvana (enlightenment), where the soul is freed from the cycle of rebirth. These teachings encourage individuals to live lives of virtue, selflessness, and spiritual awareness in preparation for a peaceful and enlightened death. In some contexts, death is seen not as a tragic event but as

1. Nacak and Erden, "End-of-Life Care," S142.

an opportunity for growth, transformation, and reunion with the divine. Preparing for death spiritually involves the following:

Acceptance and Letting Go

One of the central themes in preparing for death spiritually is acceptance. Many spiritual teachings emphasize the importance of letting go of attachments to the material world, which is seen as temporary and fleeting. The act of letting go of one's possessions, relationships, and even the body itself can be spiritually liberating. This is not a denial of the value of life or relationships but a recognition that death is part of the natural order, and holding on to worldly attachments can create suffering both for the individual and the loved ones.

Acceptance involves a surrender to the inevitable, embracing death as a natural and sacred part of the human journey. Prayer, meditation, and reflection facilitate this process of acceptance in many spiritual practices. For instance, in Christian spirituality, individuals are often encouraged to pray for a peaceful death, to seek forgiveness for past mistakes, and to trust in God's mercy. The Psalms and other Scriptures offer comfort in times of crisis, providing words of solace and reflection on the brevity of life and the hope of eternity.

As John 14:1–3 (ESV) says: "Let not your hearts be troubled. Believe in God; believe also in me. In my Father's house are many rooms. If it were not so, would I have told you that I go to prepare a place for you? And if I go and prepare a place for you, I will come again and will take you to myself, that where I am you may be also." "So, we do not lose heart. Though our outer self is wasting away, our inner self is being renewed day by day. For this light momentary affliction is preparing for us an eternal weight of glory beyond all comparison, as we look not to the things that are seen but to the things that are unseen. For the things that are seen are transient, but the things that are unseen are eternal" (2 Cor 4:16–18 ESV).

During a visit to a Buddhist patient's family at bedside, I could not say much other than providing pastoral presence and listening because of my little understanding of what end of life means for family based on religion. According to this family, Buddhism, with its focus on mindfulness and detachment, teaches that clinging to life, possessions, or identity only perpetuates suffering. Preparing for death, then, is about cultivating equanimity and preparing the mind to face death without fear. Meditation practices, particularly those focused on impermanence (*anicca*), help individuals accept the transient nature of life and develop a sense of peace in the face of inevitable death.

The Legacy of Life

Another important aspect of spiritual preparation for death is considering the legacy one leaves behind. Spiritual traditions often emphasize that our lives have meaning beyond our physical existence, and the way we live matters not only for us but also for those around us. In many ways, death gives individuals the opportunity to reflect on the lives they have led and to think about the impact they have made. Jay-Jay was a patient who, at his deathbed, could not stop asking his children to forgive him for failing them as a father due to the lifestyle he led. It could have been a miserable end of life for him, but fortunately his children came around and promised their forgiveness, held his hands, and restored peace to him.

In Christianity, preparing for death often involves reflecting on the life of service, compassion, and love that Jesus exemplified. Christians are called to love one another, forgive, and live a life of faith that reflects the values of the gospel. At the end of life, Christians may look back and ask themselves whether they have lived according to God's will, extending grace to others and building relationships based on love and respect.

For many, reflecting on their legacy is an important part of dying with peace and fulfillment. This legacy is not just about material accomplishments but also about the spiritual and emotional impact one has had on others. Preparing for death spiritually often includes a sense of gratitude for relationships and experiences, as well as a desire to leave a lasting impact of kindness, wisdom, and love.

In other religious traditions like Hinduism or Buddhism, the focus on legacy might shift toward the idea of fulfilling one's *dharma* (righteous duty) or achieving enlightenment. For Hindus, dharma is a fundamental concept in Hinduism that refers to an individual's moral duty and righteousness based on their societal role and life stage. Flood explains that dharma is central to Hindu ethics, governing personal, social, and cosmic order. He describes it as "the power that upholds the universe and society."[2] Accordingly, Olivelle highlights the relationship between dharma and the *Varnāśrama* system, which dictates social and moral duties based on caste

2. Flood, *Introduction to Hinduism*, 12–14.

(*varṇa*) and stage of life (*āśrama*). He notes that classical Hindu texts like the *Manusmṛti* outline these obligations, reinforcing the hierarchical social structure.[3]

Halbfass discusses dharma in a philosophical context, arguing that it is not merely a set of social rules but an evolving principle influenced by historical and cultural changes. He asserts that Hindu philosophy sees dharma as both prescriptive and adaptive.[4] The Bhagavad Gita, for example, teaches that fulfilling one's dharma selflessly leads to spiritual liberation (moksha). Furthermore, Klostermaier interprets dharma as the "moral backbone of Hindu thought," emphasizing its dynamic nature. He points out that Hindu scriptures, from the Vedas to the Bhagavad Gītā, offer nuanced discussions on how duty is shaped by circumstances, particularly in times of crisis.[5]

The Hope for an Afterlife

A crucial component of preparing for death spiritually is the hope for an afterlife, which provides comfort and direction in the face of mortality. The afterlife is envisioned differently across spiritual traditions, but the common thread is that it offers a sense of continuity beyond physical death. In Christianity, the hope of eternal life in heaven with God is a central theme. This belief provides individuals a deep sense of peace as they approach death. The promise of resurrection and reunion with loved ones is a source of immense comfort, and many Christians view death not as a loss but as a homecoming.

In other spiritual traditions, the concept of the afterlife is viewed in terms of reincarnation or the continuation of the soul's journey. In *Hinduism*, the soul is believed to undergo a process of rebirth, depending on the karma accumulated during life. This cycle continues until moksha is attained, when the soul is liberated from samsara. This view encourages individuals to live virtuous lives, knowing that their actions today will influence their future existences.

Even in secular spiritualities, the idea of continuity after death can offer comfort. Whether in the form of leaving a legacy, being remembered by loved ones, or simply trusting that the universe holds a place for the

3. Olivelle, *Āśrama System*, 22–25.
4. Halbfass, *India and Europe*, 310–15.
5. Klostermaier, *Survey of Hinduism*, 147–50.

individual's spirit, hope in an afterlife encourages individuals to embrace the unknown with a sense of peace.

PASTORAL ACTIONS

Pastoral actions in preparing for death centers on accompanying the dying, comforting the bereaved, and fostering a sense of hope and peace amidst grief. Some pastoral actions include:

1. **Presence and Listening:** The ministry of presence is foundational in pastoral care. Simply being with someone who is dying or grieving can provide immense comfort. Active listening allows individuals to express their fears, regrets, hopes, and memories, fostering a space of validation and healing.
2. **Spiritual Encouragement:** Offering prayers, scripture readings, or rituals aligned with the individual's faith tradition can bring solace and strength. For Catholics, sacraments such as the Anointing of the Sick or Holy Communion may be administered to provide grace and reassurance.
3. **Grief Counseling:** Pastoral caregivers can guide individuals through the grieving process, addressing feelings of anger, guilt, or despair. Pastoral caregivers can assist individuals by providing resources such as support groups, counseling, or spiritual exercises. These can help individuals navigate their loss.
4. **Community Support:** Pastoral care extends beyond the individual to the broader community. Organizing memorial services, facilitating collective mourning rituals, and encouraging mutual support among congregants help create a sense of solidarity.
5. **Education and Preparation:** Pastors can help demystify death by teaching about its spiritual significance and encouraging preparation, both practical and spiritual. Workshops on wills, advanced directives, and spiritual readiness can empower individuals to approach death with dignity and peace.
6. **Advocacy and Ethical Support:** In cases involving difficult decisions, such as end-of-life care or palliative options, pastoral caregivers can provide ethical guidance rooted in compassion and the teachings of their faith.

The above actions reflect the spiritual truth that death, though a profound loss, is also a sacred moment of transformation and hope. By addressing both spiritual and practical needs, individuals and communities are able to experience death not as an ultimate defeat, but as a passage imbued with meaning and divine presence.

FORGIVENESS AND SPIRITUAL PREPARATION

In the course of my ministry to patients, family, and staff, I have encountered people who would not let go of any wrong done to them by another. Some would not even forgive God for some misfortune they encountered in life, thereby giving up on God. Some people can't forgive themselves for their own or others' past mistakes. Understanding forgiveness would set one's mind free and also free others.

Forgiveness is a profound and transformative act that arises from a place of compassion, understanding, and personal growth. It is the conscious decision to release resentment, anger, and the desire for revenge towards someone who has caused harm or inflicted pain. Enright emphasizes that true forgiveness requires an internal transformation, in which one accepts both the pain and the humanity of the offender.[6] Forgiveness is not about condoning or forgetting the wrongdoing; instead, it involves acknowledging the hurt while choosing to let go of the negative emotions attached to it. By forgiving, individuals free themselves from the burdensome weight of grudges and attain inner peace, healing, and liberation.

Furthermore, forgiveness is an essential process that fosters reconciliation and restores damaged relationships. It requires openness, empathy, and a willingness to seek common ground. Through forgiveness, individuals open up the possibility of rebuilding trust and fostering understanding, paving the way for a renewed connection with the person who caused the harm. It is a courageous act that requires vulnerability and letting go of ego-driven desires for retribution. Ultimately, forgiveness is a powerful tool that promotes emotional wellbeing, personal growth, and the development of healthy and compassionate relationships.

In times of disagreement, forgiveness serves as the trigger for mending relationships. Many people claim they refuse to forgive their offenders because they are furious and unwilling. Others think they can never forgive because they will always remember the offense and the hurt. I understand

6. Enright, *Forgiving Life*, 45.

that when individuals are injured, they do not naturally want to forgive. However, being offended and wanting the hurt to stop might serve as inspiration for forgiving.

Obeying the scriptural command to forgive (Mark 11:25) is the first justification for forgiving. Secondly, extending forgiveness to your spouse, friend, brother, or sister facilitates reconciliation. Also, forgiveness brings emotional healing to your life and relationships by easing your sorrow and assisting you in dealing with unpleasant memories in a healthy manner. Expecting to forget anything after you have forgiven someone is unrealistic because forgiveness means remembering. It is impossible to completely erase the painful experience from your memory. Thus, Moitinho and Moitinho posit, "You will continue to remember the hurtful events because they simply cannot be erased from your mind."[7] You will always recall them, but anticipate serenity, a sense of fresh wellbeing, and the satisfaction of ending a destructive pattern of engagement with the individual.

Key Components of Forgiveness

It's important to recognize that forgiveness is a personal journey, and there is no right or wrong timeline for it. Some wounds may take longer to heal than others, and forgiveness may require ongoing effort and reflection. It's a process that varies from person to person, and each individual's experience of forgiveness will be unique. Some key components of forgiveness include:

1. **Acceptance:** Acceptance is a key component of forgiveness, as it allows individuals to acknowledge the reality of a situation and move forward without resentment. Without acceptance, forgiveness may remain superficial, as individuals may continue to hold on to past grievances. According to Worthington, a leading scholar on forgiveness, acceptance involves recognizing the hurt, understanding its impact, and choosing to release the desire for revenge or justice.[8] Through acceptance, individuals free themselves from emotional burdens and foster inner peace, making forgiveness a genuine and healing process.
2. **Empathy and Compassion:** Forgiveness often involves cultivating empathy and compassion towards the person who wronged us. This doesn't mean condoning their actions or excusing their behavior,

7. Moitinho and Moitinho, *Dream Home*, 146.
8. Worthington, *Forgiving and Reconciling*, 67.

but rather seeking to understand their perspective and recognizing their humanity.

3. **Letting Go:** Letting go allows individuals to release resentment and move forward with emotional healing. According to Smedes, "To forgive is to set a prisoner free and discover that the prisoner was you."[9] This highlights how holding on to grudges can be self-imprisoning, whereas forgiveness offers liberation. Similarly, Tutu and Tutu emphasize that "forgiving is not forgetting; it's actually remembering and not using your right to hit back."[10] This perspective underscores that forgiveness does not erase the past but rather transforms one's response to it. Letting go, therefore, is not about excusing wrongdoing but about reclaiming peace and emotional wellbeing.
4. **Healing and Reconciliation:** Forgiveness can contribute to personal healing and growth. It can help you move forward, attain closure, and restore inner peace. However, it's important to note that forgiveness does not always lead to reconciliation or rebuilding trust with the person who wronged you. Reconciliation is a separate process that may or may not be pursued, depending on the circumstances.
5. **Self-Forgiveness:** Self-forgiveness allows individuals to release self-condemnation and embrace personal growth. Without self-forgiveness, people may remain trapped in guilt and regret, hindering their ability to heal. Worthington explains that "self-forgiveness involves replacing negative, self-punishing emotions with self-compassion and responsibility."[11] This perspective highlights that self-forgiveness is not about excusing one's actions but about acknowledging mistakes and moving forward. Similarly, Enright asserts that "forgiving oneself is an act of mercy that fosters emotional well-being and inner peace."[12] By practicing self-forgiveness, individuals can cultivate resilience, foster personal transformation, and extend greater compassion to others.

9. Smedes, *Forgive and Forget*, 115.
10. Tutu and Tutu, *Book of Forgiving*, 72.
11. Worthington, *Moving Forward*, 45.
12. Enright, *Forgiveness Is a Choice*, 89.

THEOLOGICAL REFLECTION ON LIFE AND DEATH

Theological reflection on life and death is a vital process that connects faith with daily living. It bridges profound spiritual truths and the everyday realities of human existence, offering guidance, comfort, and purpose. This type of reflection helps Christians to understand how theological principles influence choices, relationships, and attitudes toward life and death. This subject is not just a theoretical exercise; it rather shapes how we live, cope, and interact with the world around us. Rooted in Scripture and faith traditions, this reflection on life and death helps Christians to confront the realities of existence with wisdom and grace.

Pastoral caregivers often find themselves at the intersection of life and death, providing support to individuals who are navigating profound physical, emotional, and spiritual transitions. Encouraging theological reflection in this context requires pastoral caregivers to first acknowledge the sacredness of their role. Life and death are profound mysteries that touch the core of human existence, and caregivers are uniquely positioned to witness and guide individuals through these moments. By fostering an atmosphere of compassion and empathy, caregivers can gently invite those in their care to reflect on the presence of God in their experiences, helping them find meaning and solace amid vulnerability.

Theological reflection on life and death also involves affirming the value and dignity of life, even in its frailest stages. This means emphasizing that every moment, whether of joy, struggle, or preparation for death is part of a divine plan. By drawing on spiritual resources such as prayer, scripture, or sacred rituals, one can explore what hope for eternal life holds for them. For instance, reading passages about God's faithfulness, such as Ps 23 or John 14:1–3, can provide comfort and a sense of divine companionship. Encouraging individuals to share their fears, doubts, and hopes makes them feel supported and find peace and assurance in God's promises.

To caregivers, one can model theological reflection by integrating their faith into their caregiving practices. Demonstrating patience, kindness, and a non-anxious presence reflects God's love and offers a tangible expression of theological truths. For instance, when facing the reality of impending death, caregivers can affirm the Christian hope in resurrection and eternal life. This encouragement does not require grand theological discourse but rather gentle reminders of God's constant presence and the enduring hope found in Christ. Through simple, heartfelt conversations, pastoral caregivers can help individuals frame their experiences within a broader spiritual perspective, offering hope and meaning.

Furthermore, families and loved ones can be encouraged to engage in theological reflection alongside the individual. Death and dying are often communal experiences, and helping families embrace these moments spiritually can provide collective healing and growth. By facilitating opportunities for shared prayer, reflection, or storytelling, pastoral caregivers can guide families in affirming their faith and celebrating the lives of their loved ones. This approach nurtures a legacy of faith that extends beyond death, offering hope and unity to those left behind. In this way, pastoral caregivers not only support individuals but also cultivate a compassionate and spiritually enriched community that reflects the love and grace of God.

Below are some practical ways to engage in theological reflection on life and death, supported by scriptural insights.

Recognizing the Sacredness of Life

One practical aspect of reflecting on life is recognizing its sacredness and purpose. From a theological perspective, life is considered as a divine gift, entrusted to individuals to steward wisely. This understanding leads to living with intentionality, prioritizing actions and relationships that align with God's will. For instance, nurturing family bonds, practicing kindness, and contributing to the wellbeing of others are all ways to honor the sacredness of life. Reflection on the teachings of Scripture, such as "I have come that they may have life, and have it to the full" (John 10:10), encourages Christians to pursue a life rich in love, faith, and service.

According to Gen 2:7, the Lord God created man from the dust of the earth and breathed the breath of life into his nostrils, transforming him into a living being. This verse emphasizes life's divine beginning and exhorts believers to respect its sacredness. Practically speaking, this entails valuing relationships, treating oneself and others with respect and love, and making decisions that are a reflection of appreciation for the life that God has given us.

Preparing for Mortality with Hope

Death is an inevitable part of life, but Scripture offers hope and perspective. Ecclesiastes 3:1–2 reminds us, "For everything, there is a season, and a time for every matter under heaven: a time to be born, and a time to die."

Acknowledging the temporality of life can inspire practical steps such as making amends, being kind and compassionate to others, and investing in what truly matters. John 11:25–26 provides reassurance, as Jesus says, "I am the resurrection and the life. The one who believes in me will live, even though they die." This hope in eternal life can comfort those facing loss or contemplating their mortality.

Reflecting theologically on death can provide a framework for confronting mortality with hope and peace. Acknowledging the inevitability of death enables individuals to focus on what truly matters, such as forgiveness, reconciliation, and leaving a legacy of faith. This viewpoint can help Christians to prepare for death, not as an end but as a transition into eternal life, fostering courage and trust in God's promises.

Finding Comfort in Grief

Grief and loss are also integral to theological reflection on life and death. When facing the loss of loved ones, theological reflection helps process grief. Psalm 34:18 says, "The Lord is close to the brokenhearted and saves those who are crushed in spirit." Practically, this means leaning on faith communities, engaging in prayer, and trusting God's presence in moments of sorrow. In the words of Robert, "No matter how many definitions there are to describe grief, the bottom line is that the pastoral care of those who are grieving is integral to the nature of human beings and deeply present in the spiritual care of those who suffer."[13] This reflection leads to seeking solace in prayer, faith communities, and rituals that honor the deceased. Sharing memories, offering acts of service in a loved one's name, participating in memorial services, reflecting on the legacies of loved ones, or engaging in moments of quiet reflection can help process grief and affirm the belief in eternal life, which can be healing.

Living with Purpose

People can be inspired to live with eternal values instead of fleeting concerns by engaging in theological reflection. Priorities can be rearranged with the aid of these goals. Priorities are reshaped when spiritual values are prioritized over material ones. Second Corinthians 4:18 says, "*Since what*

13. Roberts, *Professional Spiritual and Pastoral Care*, 313.

is seen is transient, but what is unseen is eternal, we fix our eyes not on what is seen, but on what is unseen." This inspires people to make investments in their spiritual development and build meaningful relationships.

Scripture encourages living a life of meaning and alignment with God's will. Ephesians 2:10 states, "*For we are God's handiwork, created in Christ Jesus to do good works, which God prepared in advance for us to do.*" By giving the subject some thought, believers can assess their everyday behaviors and priorities and consider how they can better serve others and carry out their divinely mandated mission. This could be tutoring, volunteering, or just being compassionate in regular conversations.

Encouraging a Legacy of Faith

Life and death reflections often lead to thoughts about legacy. Proverbs 13:22 teaches that "a good person leaves an inheritance for their children's children." Beyond material wealth, this inheritance includes spiritual values, love, and wisdom. Practically, individuals can focus on mentoring the next generation, documenting their faith journey, or contributing to causes that align with their values. Proverbs 22:6 similarly emphasizes guiding children onto the right path early in life, teaching that when they are properly directed, they are less likely to turn away later. Faith is taught through words and demonstrated through actions that mirror God's love and grace, encouraging younger generations to follow suit. By prioritizing worship, prayer, and service, families can build a strong spiritual foundation. This legacy is further strengthened by the reminder in Ps 78:4 that God's works and faithfulness should be shared with future generations so they may know His power and wondrous deeds. Such practices transform faith into a living testimony that endures and inspires generations.

Passing down a legacy of faith involves nurturing spiritual values that transcend generations, creating a foundation rooted in love, hope, and purpose. This process starts with intentional actions such as living by example and demonstrating the principles of faith in everyday life. When parents or mentors model integrity, kindness, and a deep trust in their beliefs, they inspire younger generations to embrace those values. Sharing personal faith stories, celebrating meaningful traditions, and fostering open discussions about spiritual matters can help make faith relatable and accessible. These efforts establish a personal connection to spirituality, allowing it to become more than a set of rules, transforming it into a dynamic relationship with the divine.

Engaging in Prayer and Scriptural Study

One practical approach to theological reflection is immersing oneself in prayer and Scripture. Philippians 4:6–7 offers guidance: "*Do not be anxious about anything, but in every situation, by prayer and petition, with thanksgiving, present your requests to God. And the peace of God, which transcends all understanding, will guard your hearts and your minds in Christ Jesus.*" Regular prayer and Scripture reading provide comfort and direction. Thus, reflection on life and death equips individuals to navigate these profound realities with faith, wisdom, and purpose. By grounding their reflections in Scripture and applying them to daily life, individuals find meaning in life's joys and trials while facing death with hope rooted in God's promises.

THE SACRAMENT OF THE SICK

The Anointing of the Sick, or Sacrament of the Sick, is one of the seven Catholic sacraments. It is a rite that provides spiritual and physical healing for individuals who are seriously ill, suffering from chronic conditions, or facing the end of life. This sacrament offers comfort, healing, and the strength of God's grace in times of physical or emotional distress. Though it is often associated with the final moments of life, the Sacrament of the Sick is intended for anyone who is facing significant health challenges, regardless of their age or the imminence of death. In the *Catechism of the Catholic Church*, it states: "The Church believes and confesses that among the seven sacraments there is one especially intended to strengthen those who are being tried by illness: the Anointing of the Sick. This sacred anointing of the sick was instituted by Christ our Lord as a true and proper sacrament of the New Testament."[14]

Rooted in the scriptural foundation found in Jas 5:14–15, the apostle writes, "*Is anyone among you sick? Let him call for the elders of the church, and let them pray over him, anointing him with oil in the name of the Lord. And the prayer of faith will save the one who is sick, and the Lord will raise him up. And if he has committed sins, he will be forgiven.*" This passage

14. *Catechism of the Catholic Church*, 1511.

underscores both the physical and spiritual aspects of the sacrament: the use of anointing with oil and the power of prayer for healing and forgiveness. Jesus Himself is portrayed as a healer throughout the Gospels, healing the sick and offering comfort and peace. The Church, following Christ's example, continues this ministry through the Sacrament of the Sick, extending God's healing presence to the faithful.

Larson-Miller, a theological scholar, provides a historical and theological overview of the sacrament of the sick, tracing its origins from early Christian healing practices to its formalization in the medieval and post-Vatican II Church. She explains that early Christian communities viewed anointing as a means of healing and communal support rather than solely preparation for death.[15] This practice evolved into Extreme Unction, a sacrament associated more with final absolution than physical healing. After Vatican II, the Church reaffirmed the sacrament as one of healing and spiritual strength, rather than only for the dying.[16] Larson-Miller emphasizes its dual purpose: providing spiritual grace for those suffering illness and preparing the soul if death is near.[17]

Meyendorff approaches anointing from an *Eastern Orthodox perspective*, emphasizing its role as a sacrament of both spiritual and physical healing. He explains that in Orthodox Christianity, Holy Unction (as it is called) is administered more frequently and to all believers, not just the seriously ill or dying.[18] The Orthodox tradition also maintains a strong biblical foundation for anointing, with reference to Jas 5:14–15, which calls for elders to anoint the sick and pray for healing. To this tradition, healing is a sign of the kingdom of God, a visible manifestation of divine grace that restores both body and soul. While the Catholic tradition has restored its original meaning post-Vatican II, the Orthodox Church has maintained a continuous emphasis on healing. Theologically, the Sacrament of the Sick highlights several important aspects of Christian belief, such as:

1. **God's Compassion and Healing Power:** The sacrament reflects God's compassion for the suffering and His desire to heal both body and soul. It reminds Christians that God is present in times of pain and illness, offering strength through His grace.

15. Larson-Miller, *Sacrament*, 85.
16. Larson-Miller, *Sacrament*, 85.
17. Larson-Miller, *Sacrament*, 85.
18. Meyendorff, *Anointing of the Sick*, xx.

2. **Union with Christ's Passion:** The suffering of the sick person is seen as a participation in Christ's own suffering. Just as Christ endured physical suffering for the salvation of humanity, the sick person is invited to unite their pain with Christ's passion, thereby finding meaning and purpose in their suffering.
3. **Forgiveness of Sins:** An important part of the sacrament is the forgiveness of sins. Catholics believe that illness can sometimes be linked to spiritual struggles or sin, and the Sacrament of the Sick offers an opportunity for the individual to receive forgiveness, reconciling them with God and His church.
4. **Preparation for Death:** In cases where the illness is life-threatening, the Sacrament of the Sick prepares individuals for death, offering them peace and hope in the face of the end of life. It reminds them of the Christian hope of resurrection and eternal life with God.

The Rite of Anointing

The anointing is performed using holy oil, typically blessed by a bishop during the Chrism Mass of Holy Week. The priest administers the sacrament by anointing the forehead and hands of the sick person while invoking God's grace. Accompanying prayers ask for the restoration of health if it is God's will and for the forgiveness of sins, affirming the sacrament's dual purpose of healing both body and soul. For those approaching death, the anointing provides spiritual fortification for the journey to eternal life, affirming the Christian hope of resurrection and communion with God.

This sacrament also serves as a moment of deep pastoral care and community connection. Often celebrated with the presence of family, friends, or members of the faith community, the rite embodies the collective prayer and support of the Church. It comforts the ill by showing them they are not alone in their pain but part of a larger group that shares their hopes and struggles. In this way, the Rite of Anointing not only addresses the individual's spiritual needs but also reinforces the communal nature of faith, reflecting the Church's mission to bring God's healing presence into the lives of its members.

Key Elements of the Sacrament of the Sick:

Invitation for the Sick Person

The person in need of the sacrament, or their loved ones, typically requests the anointing from a priest. The procedure can be done during a visit to the sick, in the hospital, or at the person's home.

Prayer of Faith

The priest gathers with the sick person, and a prayer of faith is said, asking for God's grace and healing. This prayer often includes petitions for spiritual healing and the strength to endure suffering.

Anointing with Oil

The priest anoints the sick person with blessed oil, usually on the forehead and the palms of the hands. The oil represents the Holy Spirit's healing power and is a symbol of strength, protection, and comfort.

The Laying on of Hands

As part of the rite, the priest may also lay hands on the sick person. This gesture signifies the transmission of the Holy Spirit and the priest's role in acting as an instrument of God's grace.

Eucharist

In some cases, the Eucharist (Holy Communion) may also be administered as part of the sacrament, particularly when the person is able to receive it. The Eucharist, as the body and blood of Christ, brings spiritual nourishment and is a source of hope and strength during illness.

Prayers for Healing

The priest prays for the sick person's healing, both spiritual and physical, according to God's will. While physical healing is desired, the ultimate prayer is that the individual's soul be healed and that they may be strengthened by God's grace to endure whatever is to come.

Who Can Receive the Sacrament?

The Sacrament of the Sick is available to any Catholic or Orthodox Tradition who is seriously ill, undergoing surgery, or dealing with significant health challenges. This includes:

- Individuals suffering from chronic illness or serious medical conditions.
- Those who are undergoing major surgery, especially when the outcome is uncertain.
- Elderly individuals whose health is in decline.
- People in danger of death due to illness or old age.

The sacrament can be received more than once, particularly if a person's condition worsens or if they recover and later experience a serious illness. The Church encourages early reception of the sacrament, rather than waiting until the person is near death, as it is meant to bring comfort and healing during the entire course of an illness, not just at its conclusion.

The Role of Family and Friends

While the Sacrament of the Sick is administered by a priest, it also involves the active participation of the sick person's family and other loved ones who are present. The pastoral caregiver and the family members and friends often play a significant role in arranging for the sacrament and providing emotional and physical support during the person's illness. The presence of loved ones at the anointing reinforces the communal and loving nature of the sacrament. Moreover, the sacrament encourages the community of faith to offer prayers, support, and comfort to the sick individual. This sense of shared prayer and solidarity helps the person to feel enveloped by the love of the Church, both spiritually and emotionally.

Summarily, the Sacrament of the Sick is a vital expression of God's love and care for those who are suffering. It is a source of spiritual healing, offering peace, forgiveness, and comfort in the face of illness and impending death. This sacrament provides a powerful reminder of God's presence and the hope of eternal life. It emphasizes the Christian belief that suffering is not without purpose and that God's grace can bring healing, peace, and transformation in the midst of life's most difficult moments. Through this sacrament, the Church continues the healing ministry of Christ, offering solace and strength to the faithful in their times of greatest need.

4

Between Faith and Medicine

(Navigating End-of-Life Dilemmas)

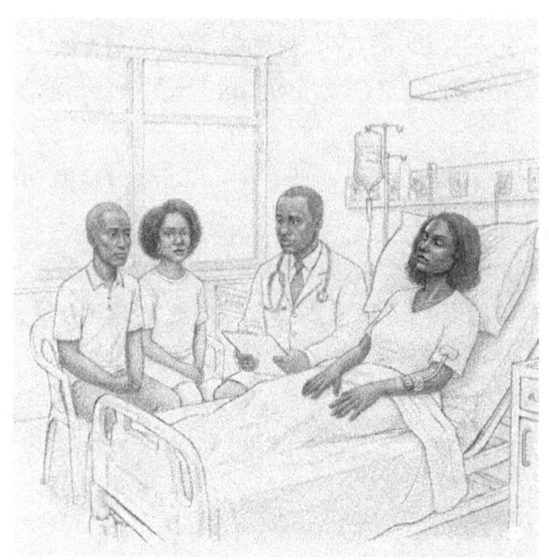

STORY 1: A STORY OF FAITH, FAMILY, AND THE SACRED TENSION BETWEEN LIFE AND LETTING GO

Upon entering a room in the ICU (Intensive Care Unit), I saw Anna lying in bed. She was fifty-eight when she suffered a sudden and devastating stroke. A once-vibrant pastor's wife, Sunday school teacher, and gardener, she now lay unresponsive in the ICU, her body tethered to machines that hummed, blinked, and breathed for her.

Her husband, Pastor Tom, stood by the window, Bible in hand. Their children, Samuel, a young doctor, and Miriam, a devout missionary, had flown in. The question they faced was one no family ever feels ready to answer: Should the machines be turned off?

Samuel, shaped by experience in emergency rooms, spoke with a trembling kind of clarity. "Dad, Mom is not coming back, not as she was. The doctors say her brain has stopped functioning. It's time to let her rest."

Miriam, eyes rimmed with red, whispered, "But God can work miracles. Don't you believe in miracles anymore?" she said, turning toward Samuel and then toward me. Tearfully, she asked, "Sr. Pam, what if God is not finished with her yet?" I could not say a word to her at that time, but drew towards her and gave her my shoulders.

Tom was silent. The weight of both their truths pressed into his heart, the clinical finality of death, and the aching hope of faith. According to Tom, that night, he prayed like he hadn't prayed since he was a young man, pacing the room, asking not for answers, but for courage.

The next day, he sat beside his wife and opened her worn Bible, its pages full of her notes and prayers. His fingers paused on a passage she had underlined years ago:

"There is a time to be born, and a time to die . . . a time to plant, and a time to uproot." (Eccl 3:2)

His voice broke as he said, "You always loved that verse, Anna. You said death was like passing through a garden gate; you didn't fear it, just hoped someone would walk with you through it."

He turned to his children. "Your mother believed that death is not the enemy, only separation is. And we believe in a God who is present in all situations."

With tears, they made the decision to let her go. Gathered in prayers, machines were silenced. The room, for the first time in days, was filled not with beeping, but with hymns and the whisper of goodbye.

Anna died holding the hand of the man she had loved for forty years. Not because they gave up on a miracle, but because they entrusted her to the greatest one of all: God's eternal mercy.

Reflection: *This story embodies the ethical and theological tension many families face: the sanctity of life vs. the dignity of death, the hope for divine healing vs. acceptance of divine timing. It invites us to see that faith is not only in the power to save, but also in the grace to surrender.*

STORY 2: THE QUIET AGREEMENT

Martin was a retired physics professor, the kind of man who believed in reason, in stars, nature, in the beauty of entropy. He didn't believe in God, afterlife, or fate, but he did believe in dignity. His daughter, Amara, had grown up in a home where questions were sacred, science was trusted, and honesty was a kind of prayer.

At eighty-four, Martin was dying of advanced ALS (Amyotrophic Lateral Sclerosis—a nervous system disease that affects nerve cells in the brain and spinal cord. ALS causes loss of muscle control, and it gets worse over time). His speech was fading, his body locked inside itself, but his mind was clear. He had always told Amara, jokingly, "If I ever become a man in a bed full of tubes, promise me you won't turn me into a project."

Now here he was, exactly that.

Amara sat with the palliative care team as they discussed options. A feeding tube? A tracheotomy? Full resuscitation in case of collapse? Each intervention could buy days, weeks, maybe months. But not meaning.

Amara and her father had developed a code when speech failed. Two blinks of eyes means "yes," and one blink "no." She looked at her father, squeezed his hand, and asked: "Do you want us to keep going with everything they're offering?" One blink—no.

Later, her brother Uche flew in. He hadn't visited in years and couldn't understand. "We can't just let Dad die," he said. "Why are we giving up too soon?"

Amara shook her head. "We're not giving up. We're listening. Dad's always believed that living isn't just breathing; it's being able to choose how you want to be in the world. He's made his choice."

"But what if we're wrong?" Uche asked.

Amara's eyes softened. "Then we'll have been wrong with love."

Martin was discharged and transitioned to comfort care at home, morphine for the pain, silence for the dignity. Amara brought him his favorite jazz records. Uche read from The Origin of Species. *They declined pastoral care, didn't pray or invoke a higher power or plan. But they stayed, wholly present, wholly human.*

Martin died one evening as "Blue in Green" played in the background, the sun painting soft light on his bookshelf. His daughter whispered, "You lived as you believed, and we honored that."

Reflection: *This story illustrates how end-of-life dilemmas are not only religious or theological; they are deeply moral, centered around autonomy, compassion, and the dignity of choice. For those with no religious tradition, the questions are no less profound: What does it mean to live well? And how do we die without regret? The answer is found, perhaps, in the same place—love, presence, and respect for the values that shaped a life.*

As a student chaplain during my residency, and hailing from a country where hospice care is rarely contemplated in end-of-life scenarios, I found it challenging to comprehend why individuals would regard hospice as a viable alternative. It seemed to me a means to expedite death. As I progressed in my training, I noticed that the objective is to alleviate the patient's discomfort and offer comfort, which necessitates the acceptance of unavoidable drug side effects.

End-of-life care presents profound ethical and theological dilemmas, as individuals, families, and healthcare providers navigate complex decisions about life, death, and the moral implications of medical interventions. One of the primary ethical challenges involves balancing the principles of autonomy and beneficence.[1] Patients may express a desire to refuse life-sustaining treatments, such as mechanical ventilation or artificial nutrition, raising questions about whether honoring such wishes constitutes an ethical obligation or a form of abandonment.[2] According to Beauchamp and Childress, medical ethics emphasize respecting patient autonomy while also considering the duty of caregivers to act in the patient's best interest.[3] The debate over physician-assisted dying further complicates this issue, as some argue that it provides a compassionate choice for terminally ill individuals, while others view it as a violation of the sanctity of life.[4]

From a theological perspective, religious traditions offer diverse interpretations of suffering, death, and medical interventions. Many Christian ethicists, for example, argue that human life is sacred and that suffering can have spiritual significance, discouraging euthanasia and aggressive

1. Beauchamp and Childress, *Principles of Biomedical Ethics*, 140.
2. Byock, *Dying Well*, 164.
3. Beauchamp and Childress, *Principles of Biomedical Ethics*, 152.
4. Callahan, *Troubled Dream of Life*, 89.

life-ending measures.[5] In contrast, some religious frameworks prioritize alleviating suffering, supporting palliative care and pain management even if it may unintentionally hasten death.[6] *Islamic perspectives* generally prohibit active euthanasia but emphasize the permissibility of withholding extraordinary treatments when recovery is unlikely.[7] *Jewish ethical thought* often considers both the preservation of life and the prevention of undue suffering, allowing certain medical decisions to be made based on the patient's condition.[8] These varying theological perspectives highlight the complexity of end-of-life decision-making, requiring sensitive engagement with both ethical principles and spiritual beliefs to ensure that care aligns with the values of the dying person and their loved ones.

On the same note, the Catholic Church upholds the sanctity of life while recognizing that death is a natural part of human existence. Ethically, it opposes euthanasia and assisted suicide but allows withholding or withdrawing *extraordinary* or *disproportionate* medical treatment if it only prolongs suffering without hope of recovery. Theologically, Catholics believe in redemptive suffering but also affirm that pain relief, even if it may unintentionally shorten life, is morally acceptable under the principle of *double effect*. Ultimately, end-of-life care should respect human dignity, provide comfort, and entrust the dying to God's mercy.

Another ethical dilemma in end-of-life care arises when family members or medical staff disagree about treatment plans or the best course of action for the patient. This can result in tension and distress, both for the patient and for those providing care. Pastoral care often plays a mediating role, helping to facilitate conversations among family members, healthcare professionals, and the dying person. The aim is to ensure that decisions are made collaboratively, with sensitivity to the emotional and spiritual needs of everyone involved. Pastoral caregivers also provide an essential role in advocating for the dying person's wishes, ensuring that they are heard and respected, while offering emotional and spiritual support during this difficult process. In addressing these ethical and theological dilemmas, the medical care team can help individuals and families navigate the complexities of end-of-life decisions, grounding them in faith and moral clarity.

5. Meilaender, *Bioethics*, 62.
6. Quill, *Physician-Assisted Dying*, 37.
7. Sachedina, *Islamic Biomedical Ethics*, 115.
8. Dorff, *Matters of Life and Death*, 142.

This chapter explores the intersection of ethics, theology, and the practicalities of end-of-life care, highlighting key dilemmas and offering perspectives to navigate these complex situations.

Autonomy vs. Beneficence

Autonomy and beneficence are two fundamental principles in medical ethics that often come into tension during end-of-life care. Autonomy refers to the right of patients to make their own informed decisions regarding their healthcare, including the choice to refuse or discontinue life-sustaining treatments. This principle emphasizes respect for the individual's freedom to determine their course of action based on their values, preferences, and beliefs. In contrast, beneficence is the obligation of healthcare providers to act in the best interest of the patient by promoting their wellbeing and preventing harm.[9] When these two principles conflict, as they often do in cases of terminal illness or life-threatening conditions, it creates a complex ethical dilemma. For example, a patient may wish to refuse treatment, even if doing so may hasten their death, which raises questions about whether it is morally acceptable to honor this decision or whether the healthcare provider has a duty to intervene in the patient's best interest.

In the context of end-of-life care, this ethical tension is particularly evident in situations where patients request life-ending measures such as physician-assisted suicide or euthanasia, which may be viewed as violating beneficence from the perspective of healthcare providers. However, proponents of patient autonomy argue that individuals have the right to choose how they want to die, particularly if they are suffering from a terminal illness.[10] Conversely, those who prioritize beneficence may argue that preserving life, even when death is imminent, is inherently part of the healthcare provider's responsibility. Byock suggests that this tension can be managed through compassionate communication, where both the patient's desires and the healthcare provider's ethical obligations are carefully considered.[11] The balance between these two principles requires careful deliberation, often involving discussions with the patient, family, and interdisciplinary healthcare team to ensure decisions align with the patient's values while also promoting their wellbeing.

9. Beauchamp and Childress, *Principles of Biomedical Ethics*, 134.

10. Quill, *Physician-Assisted Dying*, 22.

11. Byock, *Dying Well*, 159.

The Ethics of Withholding and Withdrawing Treatment

The ethics of withholding and withdrawing treatment are central issues in end-of-life care, often raising difficult moral questions for patients, families, and healthcare providers. Withholding treatment refers to the decision to not initiate or provide a medical intervention that could extend life, while withdrawing treatment involves discontinuing an ongoing intervention. The ethical dilemma arises when healthcare providers must balance the patient's right to autonomy with their duty of beneficence, which is to act in the best interest of the patient.[12] Looking at it from the perspective of autonomy, patients may choose to forgo treatment if it is aligned with their values, desires, or quality of life considerations. In this context, healthcare providers are ethically obligated to respect these decisions, even if it results in the patient's death. On the other hand, beneficence suggests that healthcare professionals should seek to promote the wellbeing of the patient, which may sometimes conflict with honoring the patient's decision to withhold or withdraw treatment.

The ethical and legal considerations surrounding these decisions are influenced by the principle of *double effect*, which holds that an action with two outcomes—one intended and one unintended—is ethically permissible if the intended effect is morally good and the unintended harm is proportionate and foreseen but not intended.[13] *For instance*, when a physician withdraws life-sustaining treatment like a ventilator, the intended goal may be to alleviate suffering, while the unintended consequence may be the patient's death. Proponents of this approach argue that it is ethically justifiable as the physician is acting to relieve suffering rather than causing death. However, some argue that withdrawing treatment can be morally problematic, especially in cases where the patient's family or healthcare agent has not explicitly consented, or when the medical team has a different interpretation of the patient's best interests. According to Beauchamp and Childress, withholding and withdrawing treatment can be morally acceptable when it aligns with the patient's informed wishes and when continuing the treatment would lead to unnecessary suffering or have no benefit to the patient.[14]

Determining when to withhold or withdraw life-sustaining treatments is a common and difficult challenge. Key questions that often arise include:

12. Beauchamp and Childress, *Principles of Biomedical Ethics*, 153.
13. Finnis, *Natural Law and Natural*, 322.
14. Beauchamp and Childress, *Principles of Biomedical Ethics*, 156.

- Is the treatment futile? Medical futility refers to interventions unlikely to achieve the desired therapeutic outcome. However, defining futility can vary based on clinical judgment and patient perspectives.
- Does withdrawing treatment differ morally from withholding it? Many ethicists argue there is no moral distinction between the two, but emotional and cultural factors often influence perceptions.

Healthcare teams must navigate these decisions with sensitivity, respecting the dignity of the patient and involving family members when making decisions.

The Role of Palliative Sedation

Palliative sedation is an ethical and medical practice used to relieve extreme refractory symptoms in patients at the end of life. It involves the use of sedative medications to induce a state of unconsciousness, allowing patients to be free from distressing physical pain, agitation, or suffering that cannot be managed by other means. This practice is generally reserved for situations where other interventions have failed to provide relief, and where the patient is experiencing unbearable suffering, particularly in the final stages of a terminal illness. The goal of palliative sedation is not to hasten death but to provide comfort and relieve suffering when all other treatment options have been exhausted.[15] This practice raises significant ethical questions regarding the balance between alleviating suffering and the potential for hastening death. While some argue that palliative sedation is ethically justifiable as a means of ensuring that patients experience a peaceful death, others raise concerns like:

- Is it ethically permissible to sedate a patient to unconsciousness if it indirectly hastens death?
- How does palliative sedation differ from euthanasia?

Listen to Sarah's Dilemma

Sarah took care of her mother when she was near death. She sat by her mother's hospital bed, her heart heavy with conflict. The doctors had recommended

15. Clark, *Ethics of End-of-Life Care*, 104.

hospice and palliative sedation *to ease her mother's unbearable pain from terminal cancer, but Sarah hesitated. Would this mean hastening her death? Was she giving up on her mother too soon? Her siblings were divided; some wanted every moment possible, while others couldn't bear to see their mother suffer. Seeking guidance, Sarah spoke with their family pastor, who reassured her that palliative sedation was morally acceptable in Catholic teaching if its intent was to relieve suffering, not to cause death. After a tearful discussion with the doctor, the family agreed. As the sedation took effect, their mother's frowned face softened, and she drifted into peaceful rest. She passed away two days later, surrounded by love, without agony. Though heartbroken, Sarah found solace in knowing they had chosen compassion over prolonged suffering.*

From an ethical standpoint, proponents of palliative sedation often invoke the principle of double effect, which allows for actions that have both good and harmful consequences as long as the harm (such as hastening death) is unintended and the good (such as relief from suffering) is the intended effect.[16] Beauchamp and Childress argue that palliative sedation can be ethically acceptable when it is used to relieve pain and suffering in a terminally ill patient, and when the sedation is not intended to cause death, but rather to improve the patient's quality of life during their final days.[17] Critics, however, point out that even though the intention is to alleviate suffering, there is still a risk that the practice may blur the lines between permissible palliative care and active euthanasia. The decision to use palliative sedation is often made with careful consideration of the patient's wishes, the family's preferences, and the healthcare team's ethical obligations, ensuring that it aligns with the patient's goals of care and the overall objective of providing comfort in the dying process.

Resource Allocation and Justice

Resource allocation and justice are key ethical concerns in healthcare, particularly in the context of end-of-life care. These issues arise when resources, such as medical personnel, equipment, and life-saving treatments, are limited, requiring difficult decisions about how to distribute them fairly and equitably. One of the central principles in bioethics, justice, calls for the fair distribution of benefits and burdens, is to ensure that no individual

16. Finnis, *Natural Law and Natural Rights*, 322.
17. Beauchamp and Childress, *Principles of Biomedical Ethics*, 162.

is unfairly disadvantaged in receiving care.[18] When resources are limited, decisions must be made about who gets treatment, who doesn't, and what type of care is best for each patient. In the context of end-of-life care, such decisions can become even more challenging as healthcare teams must balance between providing aggressive life-sustaining treatment for terminal patients and using resources to improve the quality of life for others who may have a better prognosis.[19]

The principle of justice calls for an equitable allocation of resources, yet this must also be weighed against the principles of beneficence and autonomy. For instance, when life-extending treatments are no longer effective or beneficial for a terminally ill patient, continuing aggressive intervention may be seen as an unjust use of limited healthcare resources, particularly in settings where there are other patients who could benefit more from such interventions.[20] In situations like this, many ethicists argue that the focus should shift from life-prolonging treatment to palliative care, which aims to provide comfort and dignity rather than attempting to extend life at all costs. The allocation of resources in this context must be guided by a holistic assessment of patient needs, prognosis, and the ethical implications of each treatment option. As Daniels points out, achieving justice in healthcare requires addressing disparities in care and ensuring that all patients, regardless of their financial situation, have access to necessary end-of-life care.[21]

The ethical concerns surrounding resource allocation also intersect with the theological and cultural values that shape an individual's end-of-life preferences. While some may prioritize comfort and dignity in their last days, others may seek aggressive treatment even at the expense of resources. In such cases, healthcare providers must carefully navigate the ethical principles of autonomy and justice to ensure that patients' wishes are respected while also considering the broader social implications of resource use in a healthcare system.

18. Beauchamp and Childress, *Principles of Biomedical Ethics*, 133.

19. Clark, *Ethics of End-of-Life Care*, 110.

20. Wilson, "Resource Allocation," 560.

21. Daniels, *Just Health*, 139.

PERSPECTIVES ON THE SANCTITY OF LIFE

Story: The Beans Family

The Beans family gathered around their father, Daniel, who had been on life support for weeks after a massive stroke left him unresponsive. Doctors said there was no hope for recovery, but the family was torn. Maria, the eldest daughter and a devout Catholic, believed life was sacred and should be preserved at all costs. "Only God decides when it's time," she whispered through tears. Her brother, Luis, saw their father's suffering and the machines keeping his body alive without dignity. "Dad wouldn't want this," he argued.

They sought counsel from their pastor, who gently explained that Catholic teaching honors the sanctity of life but does not require prolonging it through extraordinary means when death is near and inevitable. Life support, in this case, was no longer helping Daniel live; it was only delaying the natural process of dying.

With aching hearts, the family came to a united decision. They removed the machines and held Daniel's hands as he passed peacefully, surrounded by love and prayer. Though grief-stricken, they found comfort in knowing they had upheld both their father's dignity and their faith's deep respect for the sacredness of life.

Many religious traditions uphold the sanctity of life, emphasizing its intrinsic value as a divine gift. This belief can complicate decisions about:

- ***Discontinuing life support:*** For some, withdrawing treatment may feel like playing God, raising theological objections.
- ***Accepting death:*** Balancing faith in divine intervention with acceptance of life's natural end can create tension.

As previously mentioned, the sanctity of life is a fundamental belief in numerous theological traditions, asserting that human existence is holy and should be respected. In Christianity, Judaism, and Islam, the sanctity of life is based on the conviction that it is a divine gift. This perspective posits that every individual is fashioned in the likeness of God and that life, from conception to natural demise, ought to be safeguarded and supported. These religious traditions frequently condemn behaviors such as euthanasia, abortion, and assisted suicide, perceiving them as transgressions against divine will. The sanctity of life perspective advocates for the care, dignity, and respect of human existence, urging individuals to regard life as holy and to make decisions that reflect this belief, especially in end-of-life care.

In secular and bioethical views, perspectives on the sanctity of life can also influence debates about euthanasia, physician-assisted suicide, and end-of-life decisions. Proponents of the sanctity of life argument often oppose practices that intentionally end life, arguing that medical interventions should be aimed at preserving it, regardless of the patient's prognosis. However, some ethicists argue that the sanctity of life should not exclude consideration of quality of life, particularly when individuals face unbearable suffering and no hope for recovery.[22] For example, the right to die with dignity may be framed as an extension of the sanctity of life, suggesting that individuals have the right to make decisions about their death that align with their values and personal sense of dignity.[23] The ongoing debate centers on the tension between the intrinsic value of life and the individual's autonomy to choose their own end-of-life path, with healthcare providers playing a critical role in mediating these often competing principles.

The ethical tension between religious and secular views on the sanctity of life can present challenges, particularly in healthcare settings where decisions must be made about how to honor both the sanctity of life and individual autonomy. The medical care team plays a key role in addressing these challenges, as pastoral caregivers offer spiritual and emotional support to help patients and families reconcile their beliefs with their circumstances. Whether guiding individuals to uphold the protection of life through faith-based care or helping them make informed, autonomous decisions about end-of-life choices, the care team is expected to support individuals as they navigate the deeply personal intersection of theological, ethical, and practical considerations regarding the sanctity of life.

NAVIGATING MEDICAL INTERVENTIONS AND PALLIATIVE CARE DECISIONS

Navigating medical interventions and palliative care decisions can be a deeply complex and emotionally challenging process, often requiring a balance between medical options, ethical considerations, and the personal values of patients and their families. Often, these decisions arise in the context of serious or terminal illnesses where the goals of care may

22. Somerville, *Death Talk*, 76.

23. Beauchamp and Childress, *Principles of Biomedical Ethics*, 121.

shift from curative treatments to prioritizing comfort, dignity, and quality of life. Understanding the scope of available interventions, alongside clear communication with healthcare providers, is essential to making informed choices that align with the patient's wishes. Such interventions include:

Medical Conditions and Prognosis

The first step in navigating these decisions is obtaining a comprehensive understanding of the patient's medical condition and prognosis. This often involves discussions with a multidisciplinary team of healthcare professionals to explore treatment options and their potential outcomes. For instance, interventions such as surgeries, chemotherapy, dialysis, or advanced life-support measures may offer a chance at prolonging life but could also carry significant risks or diminish quality of life. Patients and families need to weigh these factors carefully, often guided by the principle of "shared decision-making," which ensures that medical recommendations are integrated with the patient's preferences and values. Thus, Beauchamp and Childress point out that the principle of autonomy plays a crucial role here, as patients have the right to make decisions regarding their treatment options, even if those decisions involve refusing life-extending interventions.[24]

Palliative Care

Palliative care, distinct from hospice care, can be introduced at any stage of a serious illness and focuses on alleviating symptoms, managing pain, and supporting emotional and spiritual wellbeing. Incorporating palliative care does not mean giving up on treatment but rather enhancing the patient's overall quality of life, regardless of the prognosis. Families may sometimes struggle with feelings of guilt or fear that choosing palliative care signals "giving up." However, open conversations about the goals of care can help redefine success in terms of comfort, connection, and respect for the patient's dignity.

24. Beauchamp and Childress, *Principles of Biomedical Ethics*, 103.

Legal and Ethical Considerations

Legal and ethical considerations, such as advance directives and do-not-resuscitate (DNR) orders, are also vital in navigating these decisions. Advance care planning allows patients to articulate their preferences in writing, ensuring their wishes are honored even if they lose the ability to communicate. Healthcare providers can help demystify these documents and support families in understanding their implications. At the same time, ethical dilemmas may arise when patients' wishes conflict with the perspectives of family members or healthcare providers, requiring sensitive mediation to reach a resolution.

Beauchamp and Childress note that these decisions should be guided by a balance of beneficence (acting in the patient's best interest) and respect for autonomy, with healthcare providers playing a key role in ensuring that patients and families are well informed about their options and the likely outcomes of each choice.[25] Ultimately, navigating medical interventions and palliative care decisions is a deeply personal journey, often marked by moments of uncertainty and grief. However, by prioritizing clear communication, patient-centered care, and compassionate support, individuals and families can find pathways that honor the values and dignity of the person at the heart of the decision-making process.

Honoring One's Dignity and Autonomy

Maintaining the dignity and autonomy of the dying person is essential. Even as physical capabilities decline, it is important to involve them in decisions about their care and environment whenever possible. Small acts, such as respecting their preferences for food, clothing, or visitors, even talking to them and letting them know what you are doing or intend to do, although they cannot respond, can make a significant difference.

It involves recognizing their intrinsic worth and respecting their right to make decisions about their care and final moments. Dignity in dying is closely linked to the ability to maintain personal identity, have choices respected, and receive compassionate treatment.[26] According to Byock, affirming a dying person's dignity means acknowledging their emotional, physical, and psychological needs while ensuring they feel valued and

25. Beauchamp and Childress, *Principles of Biomedical Ethics*, 158.

26. Chochinov, *Dignity Therapy*, 25.

heard.[27] This may involve allowing them to express their wishes regarding pain management, medical interventions, or the environment in which they spend their final days. When patients retain a sense of control, they are more likely to experience a peaceful and meaningful transition.

Dignity also means recognizing their individuality. Every person's experience of dying is unique, shaped by their personality, beliefs, and life story. Companions should approach each individual with curiosity and respect, avoiding assumptions or imposing their perspectives. Studies show that individuals facing death often desire the ability to choose where and how they die, as well as the people present during their final moments.[28] Kübler-Ross emphasizes that caregivers and healthcare providers should facilitate these choices by fostering open communication, ensuring informed consent, and respecting the individual's cultural and personal values.[29] By honoring the dying person's voice and choices, we affirm their humanity and their right to define their final chapter.

INTERCONNECTED PROCESS

Navigating medical interventions and palliative care decisions is a deeply interconnected process that involves the care receiver, the caregiver, and loved ones. Each group has unique roles, perspectives, and emotional needs, and the challenge lies in harmonizing these elements to ensure care aligns with the patient's values while also addressing the wellbeing of everyone involved. Open communication, empathy, and a clear understanding of goals are vital when traversing this complex terrain.

For the care receiver, the journey often involves grappling with their mortality and weighing the trade-offs between treatment options and quality of life. Patients may face profound uncertainty about the outcomes of medical interventions, such as whether a procedure will prolong life meaningfully or merely extend suffering. Palliative care offers an alternative path, focusing on symptom relief, comfort, and emotional support. However, choosing palliative care can be emotionally fraught, as it may feel like relinquishing the hope for recovery. Ensuring that the care receiver's voice remains central to decision-making is critical, allowing them to retain autonomy and dignity even in the face of illness.

27. Byock, *Dying Well*, 131.
28. Halifax, *Being with Dying*, 112.
29. Kübler-Ross, *On Death and Dying*, 47.

Caregivers bear the dual responsibility of providing physical and emotional support to the patient while managing their stress and fatigue. The demands of caregiving can be overwhelming, particularly when decisions involve life-sustaining interventions or transitioning to palliative care. Caregivers may struggle with feelings of inadequacy or guilt, especially if they perceive themselves as unable to meet the care receiver's needs or if they are uncertain about whether they are honoring the patient's wishes. Those who provide care are encouraged to seek help, counseling, and other resources that can help them navigate their roles more effectively and reduce burnout.

Loved ones, including family members and close friends, often contribute to the emotional support network and may be involved in decision-making. However, differing opinions and emotional responses can sometimes create conflict. For example, some loved ones may advocate for aggressive treatments in the hope of a cure, while others may support comfort-focused care, reflecting their coping mechanisms and beliefs about hope, loss, and healing. It is crucial to create spaces for honest dialogue where everyone can express their feelings while prioritizing the care receiver's desires.

Shared decision-making models, supported by healthcare professionals, can bridge the gaps between the needs of the care receiver, caregiver, and loved ones. These models emphasize transparent communication, compassion, and mutual understanding, helping to ensure that decisions are not only medically sound but also emotionally and ethically appropriate. In navigating these difficult choices, families and caregivers must also prioritize their own mental and emotional wellbeing, recognizing that their resilience is essential to providing compassionate and effective care.

UNRESOLVED OR COMPLEX SITUATIONS

Story: More Than the Medicine

Seventy-year-old Ms. Elena had been diagnosed with advanced heart failure. The prognosis was uncertain. Her shortness of breath kept her in and out of the hospital, and her once-vibrant personality had faded into quiet resignation. Her daughter, Angel, visited every day, asking questions the staff couldn't always answer: "Is she getting better?" "What's next?" "Why isn't she talking anymore?"

Though medications were adjusted and her vitals stabilized, something was clearly missing. Elena would stare out the window. Angel grew tense, frustrated, and exhausted. She felt invisible in the care plan. The silence between mother and daughter deepened. Chaplains stayed present and provided spiritual and emotional support.

One evening, after another emotional outburst at the nurses' station, the attending physician, Dr. Doug, took action, not with new medications, but with a family-centered conversation, calling together the medical care team in Elena's room, and with her daughter Angel present.

After the team was done with explanations and left, the chaplain asked Elena what she was afraid of. She whispered: "Being a burden. Dying in pain. Leaving my daughter alone."

Angel began to cry. "I thought you were giving up on me," she said.

The team didn't offer false promises; they offered truth with compassion. The palliative nurse explained comfort measures. The chaplain helped Elena voice her fears. The social worker offered counseling for Angel. Together, they created a care plan that included spiritual support, weekly family updates, and time for Angel to simply be a daughter again, not a caregiver lost in the unknown.

Within days, the atmosphere changed. Elena began eating again. She smiled. Angel sat beside her without tension. The emotional storm began to pass.

Reflection: *Sometimes, healing starts not with a cure, but with a conversation, when a medical team treats the heart behind the illness.*

The response to unresolved or complex situations involving ethical and theological dilemmas demands sensitivity, wisdom, and a deep commitment to both truth and compassion. The medical team often find themselves guiding individuals and families through crises that lack clear answers, where competing values, emotions, and beliefs come into tension. In such scenarios, the care team must provide not only spiritual support but also a framework for discernment and reconciliation, rooted in faith and an understanding of human complexity.

One key aspect of the medical team responses is the need for empathetic listening. Ethical and theological dilemmas often carry significant emotional weight, and those grappling with such issues may feel isolated, confused, or even judged. The care team must create a safe, nonjudgmental space where individuals can express their fears, doubts, and concerns. This requires an intentional focus on the person's lived experience, allowing them to feel heard and valued even amidst uncertainty.

Ethical and theological dilemmas often challenge established norms or doctrines, creating tension between moral principles and individual circumstances. For instance, dilemmas surrounding end-of-life care, marriage and family dynamics, or social justice issues can leave individuals feeling caught between their faith and practical realities. Pastors must navigate these tensions by drawing on the wisdom of Scripture, church tradition, and theological reflection while also acknowledging the nuanced nature of human life. Rather than presenting rigid answers, pastoral leaders can guide individuals to seek God's will through prayer, Scripture, and communal discernment, fostering a sense of shared accountability and divine guidance.

When unresolved situations persist, there is a need to acknowledge the mystery of God's plan and the limits of human understanding. Complex dilemmas often reveal that not all questions have immediate or satisfying answers. In these moments, the care team can encourage individuals to lean into their faith, trusting in God's sovereignty even when clarity is elusive. They can also help individuals and families embrace the tension of "both/and" rather than "either/or," recognizing that faith often calls believers to hold seemingly contradictory truths in balance, such as justice and mercy, or truth and grace. One can offer hope by affirming God's ongoing presence and redemptive power, even in the midst of uncertainty. They can also encourage resilience by helping individuals focus on what can be done, whether through acts of love, advocacy, or personal growth, rather than what remains unresolved. In doing so, the care team can help patients/families to see challenges not as insurmountable burdens but as opportunities to grow in faith and trust.

Ultimately, the care team responses to unresolved or complex situations must reflect the heart of Christ: loving, patient, and steadfast. By prioritizing relational care, fostering theological reflection, and guiding individuals toward hope, the care team can navigate these challenges with grace and humility, pointing others to the God who holds all mysteries and answers in His hands.

5

Naming the Silence

(The Language of Suffering, Mystery, and Presence)

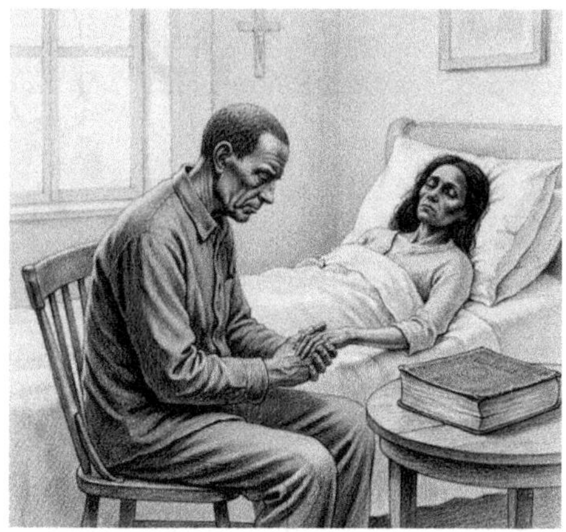

STORY: THE PRAYER THAT WASN'T PRAYED

Joseph had always been a man of words. A retired English teacher and long-time church elder, he was known in his small town for his eloquent prayers, always full of poetic Scripture, always carefully measured, always comforting. People said when Jacob prayed, heaven leaned in to listen.

But when his wife Mary was diagnosed with aggressive cancer, the words stopped coming.

In the first few weeks, he tried. He read psalms aloud at her bedside. He whispered old hymns, hoping they would hold her pain. But as her condition worsened and her body weakened, the usual prayers felt hollow. No verse seemed to fit. No phrase seemed true enough.

One morning, after a long, sleepless night, Joseph sat by her side with his Bible open but unread. He gripped her frail hand and stared out the window at the rain. For the first time in forty-two years of marriage, he had nothing to say; he stayed with her in silence.

But that moment, strangely, did not feel empty.

He did not hear a voice, nor feel a miraculous peace. He only felt a weighty stillness, as if the silence between them was being shared with Someone else. The presence was wordless, but real. It continued for days until Mary passed one afternoon.

At her funeral, Joseph stood at the pulpit. Everyone waited for a poetic tribute or a powerful prayer. But he simply said this:

"In the end, I could no longer pray the way I used to. But I have come to believe that silence can be prayer too. God heard the ache in my chest. And somehow, that was enough."

Reflection: *Joseph discovered what many pilgrims of pain eventually learn: that there is a language deeper than words. That God does not require eloquence, only honesty. In the silence of his suffering, Joseph was not abandoned; he was encountered.*

This is what it means to name the silence: to stop striving to explain it, and instead to honor it as sacred ground where God listens.

In the darkest moments of human experience, grief, illness, injustice, and death, words often falter. Suffering forces a confrontation with the limitations of language. It opens a space where silence seems more honest than speech, yet the silence itself demands naming. For pastors and caregivers walking alongside the suffering, naming this silence becomes a sacred task: not to explain it away, but to give it form, reverence, and recognition.

Suffering exposes the indescribable, the mystery that theology has long struggled to articulate. Wiesel, a Holocaust survivor and theologian, declared, "There may be times when we are powerless to prevent injustice, but there must never be a time when we fail to protest."[1] His words echo the truth that silence can be both a wound and a witness. In the face of

1. Wiesel, *Night*, 122.

immense suffering, silence may be born from reverence, but it may also be a protest, a refusal to let horror be normalized.

Naming the silence is not about removing the mystery of suffering but attending to it with theological integrity. Scripture itself provides us language that resists resolution. The book of Job, perhaps the Bible's most profound engagement with undeserved suffering, does not end with clear answers. Instead, it ends with Job silenced, standing in awe before the whirlwind. As the theologian Gutiérrez writes, "The message of the book of Job is that we must abandon the theology of retribution and open ourselves to a God who is present in the mystery."[2] When encountering the grieving or the dying, the minister does not stand as a dispenser of answers but as a witness, holding space for the sacredness of what cannot be said. Bonhoeffer, who wrote from a Nazi prison cell before his execution, reminds us, "Silence in the face of evil is itself evil: God will not hold us guiltless. Not to speak is to speak."[3] Yet for Bonhoeffer, this speaking is not always propositional; it is often relational. It is being with, not talking at.

The silence of suffering can also be a place of encounter with God. Christian mystics, from Julian of Norwich to John of the Cross, spoke of "the dark night of the soul" not as a void, but as a threshold. Here, God is not absent but hidden, veiled in mystery, and encountered through a stripped-down faith that clings to hope without clarity. As Wolterstorff writes in his moving lament after the death of his son, "I shall look at the world through tears. Perhaps I shall see things that dry-eyed I could not see."[4]

This naming of silence does not solve the problem of suffering. It honors it. It calls pastors, caregivers, and companions to walk tenderly into the quiet places of grief, not to fill them with noise but to embody the Word who became flesh, the God who entered into our suffering. In the silence of Gethsemane, in the cry of dereliction on the cross, and in the hushed stillness of Holy Saturday, we find a God who does not explain away pain but embraces it. Therefore, the pastoral task at the crossroads of mortality is not to erase the mystery but to reframe it. Silence becomes liturgical, an act of faith. In naming the silence, we do not deny the abyss, but we proclaim that even in the abyss, we are not alone.

2. Gutiérrez, *On Job*, 10.

3. Bonhoeffer, *Letters and Papers from Prison*, 289.

4. Wolterstorff, *Lament for a Son*, 26.

WHEN WORDS FALL SHORT

In the sacred spaces of hospital rooms, hospice beds, or funeral vigils, there often comes a moment when words fall short. The impulse to speak is strong; we reach for comfort, explanation, or reassurance. Yet in the presence of profound loss, pain, or mystery, silence sometimes says what speech cannot. This silence is not emptiness; it is a language of its own, a holy language that speaks when human words falter.

The cross itself, Christianity's most central symbol, does not explain suffering; it inhabits it. As Williams writes, "Good Friday is not about God's need for pain, but about God's sharing in our pain."[5] It is a silence that bears witness, not to divine indifference, but to divine intimacy. The biblical witness understands silence not as neglect, but as reverence. The story of Job illustrates this vividly. After his friends' long-winded attempts to justify God's justice, God finally speaks, not to answer, but to draw Job into deeper mystery. Job's response is not theological clarity but humility and awe: "I lay my hand on my mouth" (Job 40:4). As Gutiérrez notes, "The real answer to suffering is not a reply at all, but a presence."[6] Accordingly, Bonhoeffer, writing from a Nazi prison cell, knew the weight of unanswerable suffering. He warned that "talking too much about God during times of crisis can become a kind of betrayal."[7] Instead, true presence listens more than it speaks. It mirrors the ministry of Jesus, who wept at Lazarus' tomb before offering resurrection. The tears came first. The silence came first.

Mystics like Julian of Norwich and John of the Cross describe this experience as a "dark night of the soul," where the soul is stripped of illusions and forced to wait, not in despair, but in naked trust. Silence here is not abandonment; it is gestation. Wolterstorff said after his son's death, "What I need to hear from you is that you recognize how painful it is. I need to hear you say that you are with me in my desperation."[8] This is the ministry of presence, not propositions.

In pastoral care, then, naming the silence means acknowledging that some wounds should not be explained but witnessed. It emphasizes the theology of incarnation over articulation, focusing on being present rather than merely speaking to others. We walk with the hurting, not because we

5. Williams, *Sign and the Sacrifice*, 29.

6. Gutiérrez, *On Job*, 10.

7. Bonhoeffer, *Letters and Papers from Prison*, 289.

8. Wolterstorff, *Lament for a Son*, 34.

have answers, but because we believe in a God who chose to suffer with us. In Christ, the Word became flesh and did not flee from suffering. He was silent before his accusers. He cried out in dereliction, and he remained buried before rising.

There are moments in the ministry of care when words not only seem inadequate but also feel like an intrusion, moments at the edge of a hospital bed, in the stillness of hospice care, or in the raw silence following tragic news. In these sacred spaces, silence becomes more than absence; it becomes presence. The temptation to fill the void with explanations or reassurances often arises from our discomfort, yet silence can be more powerful than speech when ministering to the dying or grieving. In this sacred hush, pastors and caregivers offer a profound gift: not solutions, but solidarity. In doing so, they echo the presence of the One who is near to the brokenhearted. When words fall short, love does not.

BIBLICAL LAMENT AND THE HUMAN CRY

The Bible accords sacred permission to grieve, to question, and to lament. The Psalms alone contain over forty psalms of lament, many of which begin with urgent, unfiltered cries: "How long, O Lord?" (Ps 13:1), "Why do you hide your face?" (Ps 44:24). These are not blasphemies, but prayers. They testify that God is not absent from our suffering, even when God feels hidden. The book of Lamentations provides poetic form to the grief of a devastated people. Its vivid imagery, "My eyes flow with tears" (Lam 1:16), is not sanitized theology but an honest confrontation with loss. Job, too, joins this chorus of faithful lament. After the collapse of his world, he sits in silence for seven days with friends who understood, initially, that silence was the only faithful response (Job 2:13). It was when they began to speak that they erred.

The language of lament is perhaps the most honest speech in the Bible. It is the voice of anguish, protest, grief, and longing, a human cry that does not deny God but calls out to Him from the depths of suffering. In a world that often silences or sanitizes pain, biblical lament provides theological permission to express the unspeakable. It is not weakness; it is worship, raw, defiant, and faithful. The psalmist always named the reality of suffering: betrayal, abandonment, injustice, illness, and even divine silence. It is considered not the voice of doubt but of profound relationship, a faith that believes God is still listening, even when God seems absent.

Brueggemann calls lament "an act of bold faith," arguing that such speech assumes a covenantal God who can be addressed, even confronted.[9] Lament is not despair but protest grounded in hope. It is the voice of a people who still believe that God cares, that God can act, and that the relationship is real enough to handle complaint. The psalmist dares to voice sorrow, not because God has ceased to exist, but because God *must* exist for the cry to have meaning.

In pastoral ministry, lament is a sacred tool, especially in moments of death, loss, trauma, or injustice. Far from being a failure of faith, the expression of grief through lament connects the suffering heart with biblical tradition. Job laments not only his personal loss but the cosmic disorder it seems to represent. Jeremiah weeps over Jerusalem with anguish that echoes into modern cries for justice. Even Jesus, on the cross, reaches for the words of Ps 22: "My God, my God, why have you forsaken me?" (Matt 27:46). Jesus' use of lament consecrates it as divine language. In his most human moment, he chooses words from Scripture's most sorrowful place.

Lament also serves a communal function. The book of Lamentations is not the outpouring of one individual but the song of an entire people who have seen their world collapse. In this, biblical lament becomes a public theology, naming collective suffering and inviting shared mourning. In congregational settings, lament opens space for corporate grief, solidarity with the oppressed, and healing through honest liturgy. As Rah argues, "Without lament, we lose our ability to cry out against injustice."[10]

In pastoral care, encouraging lament is an act of profound respect for the human experience. It allows grievers to say, "This hurt." "The pain is not how things are supposed to be." It provides people words when their own fail. The cry of lament does not alleviate the pain, but it offers dignity and companionship in the valley of death. To lament is to believe that our tears matter to God. Lament does not end with sorrow. It often leads to new forms of solidarity, resistance, and compassion. By embracing biblical lament, the church becomes a community where tears are not hidden but held, where protest is prayer, and where the human cry is met by the mysterious, comforting presence of God.

9. Brueggemann, *Message of the Psalms*, 52.

10. Rah, *Prophetic Lament*, 21.

GOD AS A COMPASSIONATE WITNESS

In the face of human suffering, the question often arises: Where is God? While theology offers many responses—doctrinal, philosophical, and eschatological—the biblical witness returns again and again to one central truth: God is present. God is present, not as a distant observer or indifferent sovereign, but as a compassionate witness who sees, hears, and enters into the pain of creation. This is not a detached sympathy. It is a divine solidarity that dignifies human sorrow.

The Scriptures offer countless glimpses of a God who sees and stays. When Hagar fled into the wilderness, she encountered the divine not as judge but as witness. "You are the God who sees me," she proclaimed (Gen 16:13 ESV). Her suffering did not vanish, but it was seen. This seeing is not passive observation. It is compassionate attention, the kind that hears the cry, holds the wound, and honors the grief. Fretheim captures the concept when he says, "God is not untouched by the world's suffering; God suffers with."[11]

To speak of God as a compassionate witness is not to minimize divine power but to deepen our understanding of divine presence. God is not always the voice that breaks the silence; sometimes God is the silence that breaks the loneliness. Jesus Christ, in his passion, becomes the clearest expression of this divine companionship. He weeps, he bleeds, he remains. On the cross, he speaks just seven short sentences, then enters the silence of death itself. However, even in his silence, God is speaking. As Moltmann observes, "The God who cannot suffer is poorer than any man. For a God who is incapable of suffering is a being who cannot be involved."[12] In Christ, God is involved. The incarnation shows that God doesn't just watch pain from a distance; he enters it, lives it, and dies through it. This is not a theology of explanation; it is a theology of witnessing presence.

Pastorally, this knowledge reshapes our role. When words fail, as they often do in the presence of trauma, death, or grief, we are not called to fill the silence with noise. We are called to mirror God's compassionate witness. We sit beside the suffering not to offer answers, but to embody attention. We do not preach in every moment. Sometimes we hold a hand, whisper a prayer, or simply remain. In those moments, our silence becomes sacramental.

11. Fretheim, *Suffering of God*, 9.

12. Moltmann, *Crucified God*, 222.

The Psalms reinforce this ministry of witness. "You have kept count of my tossings; put my tears in your bottle," says Ps 56:8. It is an astonishing image; God not only notices pain but also collects it, stores it, and remembers it. No suffering is lost on God. No tear evaporates unnoticed. The divine witness is meticulous in mercy. In the valley of the shadow, then, we are not alone. The God who watched over Hagar, wept with Mary, and cried out from the cross now watches, weeps, and cries with us. To name the silence is not to declare God's absence; it is to trust God's mysterious presence even when unspoken. God witnesses the silence, and in doing so, makes it holy.

SUFFERING AND REDEMPTIVE MEANING

Story: Grace in the Pain

Chi was a vibrant woman in her fifties when she was diagnosed with terminal cancer. As the pain grew worse, her friends urged her to ask for stronger medication or even consider palliative sedation. But Chi, a woman of deep faith, gently declined. "This suffering," she said, "I offer it up for my children, for those who are alone, for souls who need grace."

Her pastor visited often, praying with her and encouraging her to unite her suffering with that of Christ on the cross. Chi found strength in that connection, believing her pain had purpose, even if unseen. Her family struggled at first, wishing she would ease her agony, but over time, they witnessed the quiet peace and deep compassion she radiated, even in her weakest moments.

When Chi passed, her room was filled with prayer, love, and a strange sense of peace. Her children later said that her final weeks had taught them more about faith, love, and courage than anything else ever could. Her suffering, though painful to watch, had become a silent sermon of redemptive grace.

Suffering is an inevitable aspect of human existence, yet many religious and philosophical traditions offer ways to ascribe meaning to it, particularly through the lens of redemption. In Christianity, suffering is often understood as a means of participating in the passion of Christ. The apostle Paul wrote about rejoicing in sufferings, believing that they produce perseverance, character, and hope (Rom 5:3–5). From this perspective, suffering is not meaningless; instead, it is an opportunity for spiritual growth, purification, and deeper reliance on God. By uniting their pain with Christ's sacrifice, believers may obtain comfort and purpose in their struggles, seeing them as part of God's greater plan for redemption and transformation.

In secular contexts, redemptive meaning can also be found in how individuals interpret and respond to their suffering. For many, the process of grappling with terminal illness can lead to important personal insights, such as the reconciliation of broken relationships, the reaffirmation of life's purpose, or the deepening of connections with loved ones.[13] The idea of suffering as redemptive is closely tied to the concept of resilience, where individuals find strength in adversity and seek to create meaning out of their pain. This is especially significant in end-of-life care, where patients may be encouraged to reflect on their lives, make peace with past regrets, and find comfort in the knowledge that their suffering is part of a larger, perhaps spiritual, journey. Beauchamp and Childress assert that the emotional and existential aspects of suffering must be recognized in the care of terminal patients, advocating for holistic strategies to mitigate suffering that address both physical and emotional needs.[14] Through this lens, suffering is not seen as an end but as part of a larger narrative that can lead to healing, whether spiritually, emotionally, or relationally.

According to Christian doctrine, suffering is not meaningless but can lead to greater intimacy with God, purification of the soul, and a more profound understanding of God's love. The apostle Paul, for example, writes in Rom 8:18 that "the sufferings of this present time are not worth comparing with the glory that is to be revealed to us," implying that suffering has a transformative and eschatological purpose.[15] This understanding gives believers the strength to endure hardship, knowing that their suffering is not final and that it has the potential to be part of a larger narrative of spiritual growth and redemption.

The promises of hope and resurrection offer comfort and reassurance to those grappling with the reality of suffering and death, affirming that God is with His people during their struggles. This divine presence, described as the Holy Spirit, offers comfort, strength, and peace in the midst of pain. Christians view the resurrection of Jesus Christ as the ultimate triumph over death and suffering, offering believers the hope of eternal life beyond death. Jesus' resurrection assures Christians that death is not the end and that there is the promise of new life, free from pain and sorrow.

13. Gabel, *Finding Meaning in Suffering*, 112.

14. Beauchamp and Childress, *Principles of Biomedical Ethics*, 98.

15. Craig, *Reasonable Faith*, 120.

This belief in resurrection is not limited to Jesus alone but extends to all believers, as Christians are promised a bodily resurrection at the end of time (1 Cor 15:20–22).

For those facing terminal illness or the death of loved ones, this promise of resurrection offers profound hope and solace, as it reaffirms the idea that death does not have the final word.[16] In this light, suffering transforms into a temporary condition that believers will overcome in the eternal life that awaits them. The promise of resurrection provides a sense of hope that transcends the pain of present circumstances, offering a vision of restoration and eternal peace. In this way, Christian theology frames suffering not as a meaningless tragedy but as something that, through God's grace, can be transformed into a pathway to eternal life and joy.

Pastorally, helping individuals find meaning in suffering is a vital aspect of spiritual and emotional support. Caregivers can guide individuals in reflecting on their experiences of pain, loss, or illness, helping them to see how these challenges might lead to spiritual insight, personal growth, or a deeper connection with their faith. By creating an environment that promotes meaning and hope, pastoral caregivers empower individuals to confront suffering with courage and resilience. While not all suffering can or should be explained, offering a perspective that acknowledges the possibility of redemptive meaning can bring comfort and hope, even in the most difficult circumstances.

In some theological frameworks, suffering at the end of life is imbued with meaning, seen as a path to spiritual growth or solidarity with others. However, this view can:

- Lead patients or families to reject palliative interventions, fearing they diminish the spiritual value of suffering.
- Conflict with secular ethical commitments to minimize pain and distress.

Healthcare teams can listen empathetically to these beliefs while offering compassionate care that honors the patient's dignity. Just as God is silently present to Jesus during his agony on the cross, he is also silently present to everyone who suffers.[17] Like Jesus, Martelli emphasizes the need for caregivers to always remember that people going through suffering need love, not logic. "They need someone to sit and weep with them, not

16. Wright, *Surprised by Hope*, 155.

17. Ryan, *God and the Mystery*, 230.

to present a sermon."[18] Thus, from this divine accompaniment, hope emanates.[19] Therefore, Rom 12:12 encourages believers to be joyful in hope, patient when afflicted, and pray fervently. Thus, "the language of hope is rooted in God and God's infinite love."[20]

THE ART OF PRESENCE

Story: The Presence

Clara was a volunteer who was assigned to sit with Mr. Jensen in hospice. She had been told her job was simple: be present. No medicine to give, no therapy to administer, just presence.

Mr. Jensen was eighty-four. A retired piano teacher with no remaining family, he was thin, quiet, and already drifting somewhere between here and there. Clara had expected conversation, maybe even stories, but all she found was silence, as was described when she took up the job. He barely spoke, only nodded when she greeted him. She stayed anyway.

Each day, she returned. She brought a book and read aloud, even when his eyes were closed. She brought a small radio and played soft music, guessing it might mean something to him. She held his hand when he seemed restless. She spoke to him gently, as if every word could anchor him to something warm.

Days passed into weeks. One afternoon, after reading a few lines of poetry, she heard his voice for the first time. Barely a whisper.

"You stay," he said, not questioning, just observing.

"Yes," she replied with excitement.

And that was it. But that one word became many in the days that followed. He told her about his wife who died young, about the students who made him proud, about the piano he never sold, even when money got tight. His eyes would close in the middle of a sentence, and she would sit in the quiet, letting the silence be full instead of empty.

The day he died, he did not speak. But as the sky outside softened into sundown, he reached for her hand. His grip was faint, but steady. Clara stayed until the last breath left his chest like a sigh, and she kept holding on even after.

18. Byrne-Martelli, *Memory Eternal*, 45.
19. Zylla, *Roots of Sorrow*, 143.
20. Zylla, *Roots of Sorrow*, 143.

Reflection: *To accompany a suffering and dying person is not to fix or to save, but to witness, to honor their journey by walking the last steps beside them, in quiet love and steadfast presence. It is a sacred act of listening, holding space, and reminding them they are not alone.*

Presence goes beyond physical proximity; it involves offering undivided attention and a calm, accepting demeanor. The dying often experience a range of emotions, including fear, sadness, and sometimes relief. Rather than focusing on finding the perfect words or attempting to alleviate all suffering, the art of presence emphasizes deep listening, silent companionship, and an openness to the emotions of the dying individual.[21] Nouwen describes presence as "a gift of self," where one's attentive presence allows the dying person to feel valued, heard, and understood, even when words fail.[22]

Studies in palliative care suggest that a calm and accepting presence can ease anxiety and fear for the dying, creating a sacred space for reflection and peace.[23] This form of support does not necessarily require verbal communication; simple gestures such as holding a hand, maintaining eye contact, or sitting quietly can provide immense comfort. As Byock posits, the dying process is not just a medical event but a deeply human experience that calls for emotional and spiritual accompaniment.[24] The art of presence, therefore, involves letting go of the need to "fix" or control the situation and instead embracing the vulnerability and sacredness of the moment.

ADDRESSING EMOTIONAL NEEDS

Emotions play a significant role in the dying process. For the individual facing death, there may be moments of fear: fear of pain, of the unknown, or of leaving loved ones behind. There may also be grief for what is being lost, from physical independence to future possibilities. Anger, regret, and guilt may surface as they reflect on unresolved issues or relationships and a longing for reconciliation.[25] Addressing the emotional needs of this individual involves providing reassurance, comfort, and a sense of connection. Offering emotional support requires deep listening, empathy,

21. Byock, *Four Things That Matter*, 102.
22. Nouwen, *Wounded Healer*, 39.
23. Halifax, *Being with Dying*, 67.
24. Byock, *Dying Well*, 85.
25. Kübler-Ross, *On Death and Dying*, 45.

and a willingness to be fully present without trying to "fix" or minimize their emotions. According to Byock, acknowledging a dying person's feelings and validating their experiences can provide immense relief, helping them attain peace and closure.[26] Helping the individual focus on cherished memories, their legacy, or the love they have shared can bring a sense of fulfillment and contentment.

Companions can provide emotional support by acknowledging these feelings without minimizing or dismissing them. Phrases like "It's OK to feel this way" or "I'm here with you" can validate their experience and make them feel more connected. Encouraging conversations about regrets or unfinished business can help the dying person attain closure, whether by offering forgiveness, seeking reconciliation, or sharing unspoken thoughts with loved ones. Kübler-Ross emphasizes that emotional support should be tailored to the individual's unique experience, ensuring that their final moments are filled with love and respect.[27] Whether through verbal reassurances, gentle touch, or simply sitting in silence, addressing emotional needs plays a crucial role in easing the transition from life to death.

SUPPORTING SPIRITUAL NEEDS

The spiritual dimension of dying often takes on profound importance. Many people turn to their faith, beliefs, or sense of connection to something greater during this time. For some, this period might involve traditional religious practices such as prayer, sacraments, or rituals. For others, it could mean exploring existential questions about the meaning of life, the legacy they leave behind, or the nature of what comes after death. Many individuals facing death experience existential questions, and offering them a space to express these concerns can provide significant comfort.[28] The care provider can affirm these spiritual needs and facilitate the conversation in ways that respect the individual's beliefs and preferences. This might include arranging visits from spiritual leaders, reading sacred texts, or simply creating opportunities for quiet reflection and meditation.

For those without a defined spiritual framework, care providers can help by encouraging an emotional attachment to the broader human experience. This could involve encouraging creative expression, spending time

26. Byock, *Dying Well*, 89.

27. Kübler-Ross, *Wheel of Life*, 110.

28. Puchalski et al., *Making Health Care Whole*, 85.

in nature, or reflecting on the love and relationships that have shaped their lives. Ultimately, the goal is to help the dying person find meaning, peace, and a sense of completion. As Byock notes, spiritual support is not limited to religious practices but includes creating an environment that promotes connection, love, and forgiveness, all of which can help a dying person find inner peace.[29]

Providing spiritual care also involves respecting and honoring the dying person's beliefs, whether religious or secular. Some may obtain solace in prayer, scripture readings, or sacred music, while others may seek peace through nature, meditation, or conversations about their life's meaning.[30] Kübler-Ross emphasizes the importance of allowing individuals to express their spiritual concerns without imposing external beliefs or judgments.[31] Creating an environment of acceptance and openness ensures that the dying person feels supported in their journey, regardless of their spiritual background. By addressing these needs with compassion and sensitivity, caregivers help provide comfort and a sense of closure, making the transition from life to death more peaceful and meaningful.

RITUALS AND FAREWELLS

Rituals and farewells play a crucial role in the dying process, providing structure, meaning, and emotional closure for both the dying person and their loved ones. These rituals can be personal, familial, or culturally prescribed, serving to honor the life of the individual and ease their transition.[32] These rituals may take the form of lighting candles, saying prayers, or sharing stories, which can help create a sense of closure and connection for both the dying person and their loved ones.

Farewells are another vital part of this journey. Encouraging and facilitating these moments allows for the exchange of love, gratitude, and forgiveness. Simple acts, like expressing love, sharing a hug, or recalling shared experiences, bring comfort and healing. These goodbyes, while painful, often become cherished memories for those who remain. Byock affirms these expressions by emphasizing that these simple yet intentional acts, or even playing meaningful music, can be deeply comforting and

29. Byock, *Dying Well*, 118.

30. Koenig, *Spirituality in Patient Care*, 67.

31. Kübler-Ross, *On Death and Dying*, 92.

32. Walter, *The Revival of Death*, 83.

affirm a person's sense of belonging in their final moments.[33] These symbolic gestures and practices provide an opportunity for emotional connection and reconciliation.

Cultural and individual preferences shape how rituals and farewells are conducted. Some cultures emphasize communal gatherings, where extended family and friends visit to offer support and say their goodbyes, while others value private, intimate moments with only close family members.[34] Halifax highlights that in many traditions, rituals surrounding death aim to ease not only the transition of the dying but also the grief of those left behind.[35] In modern palliative care settings, personalized rituals, such as creating legacy projects or memory books, allow individuals to leave an enduring mark on their loved ones. Honoring these rituals and farewells provides comfort, continuity, and a sense of completion, making the end-of-life experience more meaningful.

To summarize this chapter, let us say that accompanying the dying is a profound act of love and service. It is a journey that challenges us to confront the realities of mortality while embracing the beauty and depth of human connection. By being present, addressing emotional and spiritual needs, honoring dignity, and caring for ourselves, we can offer meaningful support during one of life's most significant transitions. In doing so, we provide comfort to the dying and deepen our own understanding of life, death, and the bonds that unite us all.

33. Byock, *Four Things That Matter*, 53.

34. Stroebe et al., *Handbook of Bereavement*, 126.

35. Halifax, *Being with Dying*, 132.

PART II

At the Crossroads

6

When Love Stays

(Caring for the Living Amid Dying)

STORY: THE QUIET HOURS

Angie had always been the strong one in her family, the kind of person who remembered everyone's birthdays, showed up early with food when someone was sick, and sent handwritten thank-you notes for even the smallest gestures. But when her mother, Rosa, was diagnosed with early-onset Alzheimer's, strength took on a new meaning.

At first, it was small things: misplaced keys, forgotten appointments. But slowly, her mother, once a vibrant woman who sang while gardening and recited poetry from memory, began to fade behind clouded eyes. Angie became her caretaker, her anchor.

Every evening, after putting her own two kids to bed, Angie would drive across town to sit with her mother. One rainy night, Rosa turned to her and asked, "Are you my sister?"

Angie swallowed hard. "No, Mama, I'm your daughter, Angie." Rosa studied her face.

"Angie . . ." she repeated, slowly. "That's a beautiful name." Then she smiled, a rare, true smile. "I think I like you." It broke Angie's heart and healed it at the same time.

Eventually, Rosa forgot how to speak altogether. But Angie still came. She brushed her mother's hair, rubbed lotion into her hands, and whispered stories into the silence. Her siblings, once distant, began visiting more. They started cooking together, laughing, crying. They didn't try to fix anything, they just showed up. And in those quiet hours, something changed.

The family grew softer, closer, more present. The illness had taken so much, but it gave them this: the reminder that love isn't in the big, grand gestures; it's in the choosing to be there, to hold a hand, to remember, when someone else cannot.

Reflection: *Sometimes, support doesn't look heroic. It looks like doing the same quiet thing every day, even when no one sees. It's patience when you want to rush, grace when words fail, and presence when the future feels uncertain. In the end, love isn't just how we celebrate someone; it's how we carry them, gently, through the hardest parts.*

Supporting families and loved ones through challenging times, especially during illness, loss, or other crises, is an essential aspect of caregiving. Families often face emotional, physical, and spiritual strain when navigating these difficult situations, and their need for guidance, support, and understanding is paramount. The role of caregivers, whether family members, friends, or professionals, extends far beyond providing physical care; it also encompasses offering emotional resilience, creating spaces for meaningful conversations, and helping families maintain a sense of unity and hope amid uncertainty. This chapter investigates the various aspects of supporting families and loved ones, offering practical insights, emotional support strategies, and spiritual considerations to help individuals provide compassionate care in times of distress. Supporting families and loved ones through times of sickness, dying, and crisis is not merely compassionate; it's essential to holistic care.

UNDERSTANDING THE EMOTIONAL LANDSCAPE

Families and loved ones are often thrust into difficult circumstances with little preparation, which can lead to a range of emotions: fear, anger, grief, guilt, and confusion. The initial shock of an illness diagnosis, the approaching death of a loved one, or a sudden crisis can leave families in a state of emotional turmoil. Understanding that these emotional reactions are natural and valid is the first step in supporting them effectively.

Some of the key roles of caregivers are to provide practical assistance, such as compassionate presence, and offer a space where family members feel safe to express their emotions without fear of judgment. Listening is crucial in this process; sometimes, the best support is simply being there to listen as loved ones vent their frustrations and confusions or share their anxieties. Caregivers should also encourage healthy emotional outlets such as talking, journaling, or seeking professional counseling. Recognizing the emotional toll of caregiving, especially in cases of chronic illness or terminal conditions, is equally important. Caregivers may experience "compassion fatigue" or burnout. To be able to provide adequate support, it's vital to ensure that those who provide care receive their own emotional support, respite care, and self-care.

Providing Practical Assistance

In addition to emotional support, families often require practical assistance. This can range from help with daily tasks like meal preparation, transportation, or household chores to navigating the healthcare system and managing medical care. Family, friends, and caregivers can play a vital role in coordinating these aspects, helping to alleviate the burden on the patient/family and create space for them to focus on medical, emotional, and spiritual wellbeing. In the case of families facing end-of-life decisions, helping them to understand medical terminology and options can be invaluable. Caregivers can act as mediators between the family and healthcare providers, ensuring that the family's concerns and preferences are communicated clearly. Additionally, helping families with logistical tasks such as financial planning, making funeral arrangements, or organizing support networks can reduce stress during an already overwhelming time. It is also essential to acknowledge the varying capacities of family members; some may be able to take on more tasks, while others may need to step back or focus on offering emotional care. A strong, collaborative approach to caregiving ensures that everyone's strengths are utilized and that the family remains supported as a whole.

Fostering Communication and Unity

During difficult times, communication can become strained, with family members sometimes experiencing conflict over care decisions, roles, or differing opinions on what is best for their loved ones. Families benefit from clear, compassionate, and truthful conversations about prognosis, options, and expectations.[1] Conversations should be gentle and compassionate, providing opportunities for family members to discuss their feelings of helplessness, sadness, or anger without the pressure to "stay strong" for the sake of the loved one. At the same time, it is equally important to facilitate discussions about the loved one's wishes, end-of-life plans, and any final moments they hope to share together. This can be facilitated through regular family meetings, where everyone is provided an opportunity to voice their thoughts and concerns. A neutral party, such as a counselor, spiritual advisor, or healthcare professional, can sometimes help mediate these discussions to ensure that every voice is heard and that solutions are reached collaboratively.

Healthcare professionals can play a crucial role in facilitating family meetings that address not only medical questions but also emotional dynamics. These meetings provide opportunities for shared understanding, conflict resolution, and mutual support.[2] Importantly, family members must be given permission to express conflicting feelings, love and anger, hope and fear, and faith and doubt, without judgment. It's important for caregivers to emphasize the need for unity in the face of adversity. Reminding family members of the shared goal of providing the best care and support for their loved one can help ease tensions. Additionally, creating

1. Gawande, *Being Mortal*, xx.
2. Meier, "Family Meetings," 915–20.

opportunities for bonding and positive experiences, such as shared meals, family rituals, or moments of relaxation, can strengthen relationships and help families remain connected even amidst crisis. When conflict arises, caregivers should encourage patience, empathy, and compromise, always keeping the wellbeing of the loved one at the center of the conversation.

The Power of Presence

While there is often a desire to "fix" the situation, one of the most powerful responses is the ministry of presence. Nouwen, in *The Wounded Healer*, describes these activities as a form of spiritual care that involves simply being with someone in their suffering, without attempting to control or resolve it.[3] This form of accompaniment creates space for honest emotion and validates the experience of grief. In moments of acute illness or dying, families may need a space to cry, ask unanswerable questions, or simply sit in silence. Providing this safe space can become a spiritual and emotional anchor. As Brown has emphasized, empathy fuels connection and is the antidote to shame and isolation.[4] A caregiver's nonjudgmental presence often becomes the most remembered and cherished act of support.

Spiritual and Psychological Support

Spiritual care is often an essential aspect of supporting families during times of crisis. Offering spiritual guidance, whether through prayer, meditation, or rituals, can give families the strength and comfort they need to make tough choices. In the case of families who share a faith tradition, engaging in communal prayers, seeking spiritual counseling, or participating in religious services can promote a relaxed atmosphere and connection to a higher power. Puchalski and colleagues have argued for the integration of spiritual care in healthcare settings, particularly in palliative and end-of-life contexts. They note that addressing spiritual needs is not merely an act of kindness but a component of whole-person care.[5] Even for those who do not adhere to a particular religion, exploring existential questions about life, suffering, and purpose can provide valuable emotional support.

3. Nouwen, *Wounded Healer*, 39.
4. Brown, *Power of Vulnerability*, xx.
5. Puchalski et al., "Improving the Quality of Spiritual Care," 885–904.

Psychological support also plays a critical role. Families may face feelings of guilt, helplessness, or depression as they witness their loved one suffering or as they make difficult end-of-life decisions. Offering access to professional counseling, whether individual therapy, family therapy, or grief support groups, can provide tools to cope with these emotions. Cognitive-behavioral strategies, mindfulness practices, and stress-relief techniques can be introduced to help families navigate their emotional challenges. Encouraging self-care practices, such as taking breaks, engaging in physical activity, or connecting with support networks, can also be beneficial for reducing the psychological strain on caregivers. Support must be attuned to the cultural, religious, and spiritual frameworks that shape how individuals interpret suffering, dying, and caregiving. Some cultures emphasize communal decision-making and interdependence, while others prioritize autonomy and privacy. Spiritual beliefs may interpret illness as a test of faith, a divine mystery, or a spiritual journey.[6]

Honoring the Legacy of Loved Ones

A vital aspect of supporting families is helping them to honor the legacy of their loved ones, especially in the case of terminal illness or death. This can involve facilitating conversations about the person's life story, values, and wishes. The need to create meaningful rituals or memories, such as writing letters, sharing stories, or crafting a memory book, can provide a sense of closure and continuity. For some, expressing gratitude and love through tangible acts, such as creating artwork, planting a tree, or organizing a celebration of life, can offer comfort and meaning.

In cases of ongoing illness, caregivers can help families create opportunities for loved ones to feel valued and heard. Encouraging activities that strengthen relationships, such as making time for conversation, shared experiences, or recalling happy memories, can allow the person receiving care to feel that their life has meaning and purpose, regardless of the circumstances.

Summarily, supporting families and loved ones through difficult times is an intricate process that requires patience, empathy, and commitment. By addressing their emotional, practical, spiritual, and psychological needs, caregivers can ensure that families experience a sense of unity, hope, and strength as they face the challenges ahead. Effective caregiving not only

6. Sulmasy, "Spiritual Issues," 749–54.

involves tending to the immediate needs of the loved one but also creating an environment where families can lean on one another, obtain comfort, and navigate the complexities of illness, grief, and loss with compassion. The role of the caregiver, whether professional or familial, is indispensable in helping families remain resilient and connected during times of profound hardship. Thus, the act of supporting loved ones through sickness and death calls for presence, empathy, cultural sensitivity, and ongoing care. Whether one is a healthcare provider, spiritual leader, friend, or family member, the invitation remains the same: to walk alongside those who grieve, to listen deeply, and to affirm that they are not alone.

HELPING FAMILIES NAVIGATE ANTICIPATORY GRIEF

Anticipatory grief is a unique and often overlooked form of grief that occurs before an impending loss, such as when a loved one is facing a terminal illness or significant life-threatening condition. Families may grieve the slow loss of their loved one's identity, capacities, or role in the household. This kind of grief is frequently unacknowledged or misunderstood, leaving family members emotionally isolated.[7] Unlike traditional grief, which is experienced after a loss, anticipatory grief involves complex emotional responses as family members and loved ones process the impending reality of death or change. It can manifest in a wide range of emotions, including sadness, anger, anxiety, guilt, and even relief, as families come to terms with what lies ahead. Helping families go through this phase requires sensitivity, support, and guidance, as they confront the painful reality of an anticipated loss while also managing the emotional, physical, and psychological strain that accompanies it.

One of the first ways to assist families in navigating anticipatory grief includes:

Acknowledgment and Validation

Many families may not even recognize that what they are experiencing is a form of grief, especially when the loss has not yet occurred. Caregivers and counselors should normalize these feelings and encourage family members to express their emotions without shame or guilt. Acknowledging

7. Rando, *Anticipatory Grief*, xx.

that anticipatory grief is a natural response to the reality of impending loss allows families to give themselves permission to grieve before actual death. This can reduce feelings of confusion or isolation, as family members understand that their emotional responses are valid, even if the loss has not yet occurred.

Provide Information and Education

Providing information and education is another critical role for caregivers and healthcare providers. Families experiencing anticipatory grief may be unsure of what to expect as the illness progresses, and their uncertainty can lead to heightened anxiety or fear. Offering clear, compassionate explanations about the disease trajectory, treatment options, and possible physical and emotional changes can help families prepare mentally and emotionally for what lies ahead. This allows them to anticipate the needs of their loved one and adjust to the shifting roles they may have to assume, such as providing physical care or making difficult medical decisions. Knowing what to expect can lessen the fear of the unknown and help families approach the situation with a sense of readiness, even as they continue to grieve.

Recognize and Honor the Opportunities for Connection

It is equally important to help families recognize and honor the opportunities for connection that still exist during anticipatory grief. Despite the limited time the loved one has left, families can concentrate on creating meaningful memories together. Encouraging family members to share stories, express love, and engage in rituals or traditions can help them feel a sense of purpose and closeness during a time of sorrow. Anticipatory grief offers a unique opportunity to reflect on the legacy of the person they are losing, celebrate their life, and create lasting memories that will endure after their passing. These moments of connection can help mitigate the overwhelming sadness and promote a relaxed atmosphere as families prepare for the inevitable loss.

Provide Emotional Care

An additional crucial aspect of assisting those with anticipatory grieving is the necessity for emotional support for all parties concerned. Caregivers frequently encounter burnout or fatigue as they deliver physical assistance while simultaneously navigating the emotional burden of impending mourning. Providing respite care, counseling services, and self-care tools is crucial for sustaining the welfare of individuals in caring positions. Moreover, families ought to be urged to pursue professional counseling or grief support groups, since these options can offer a secure avenue for articulating their emotions and acquiring strategies to manage their loss effectively. Peer support, particularly from individuals with analogous experiences, can offer families solace and reassurance as they collectively navigate anticipatory sorrow.

Summarily, anticipatory grief is a challenging but natural response to the reality of an impending loss. Helping families navigate this emotional terrain requires a holistic approach that addresses the emotional, practical, and spiritual needs of all involved. By validating feelings, fostering open communication, providing information, and offering emotional and spiritual support, caregivers and professionals can help families cope with the complexity of anticipatory grief. This compassionate support not only assists families in managing the pain of impending loss but also empowers them to cherish the time they have left with their loved one, ultimately helping them prepare for the inevitable loss in a way that honors both their loved one and their own emotional journey.

RITUALS AND PRACTICES FOR SAYING GOODBYE

Saying goodbye is an inevitable part of the human experience, whether it comes in the form of death, separation, or transition. Rituals and practices for saying goodbye serve as powerful tools for individuals and families to honor and express their emotions during these difficult moments. These rituals, which can be religious, cultural, or personal in nature, provide a framework for acknowledging the significance of the moment and offering closure. Whether the goodbye is anticipated, as in the case of terminal illness, or sudden, as with an unexpected loss, rituals help those involved cope with their emotions, honor their relationships, and identify ways to navigate the grief process. Some of these rituals include:

Funeral Rites and Memorial Service

One of the most commonly practiced rituals for saying goodbye is the funeral rite and memorial service, which plays a significant role in marking the transition from life to death. Funerals, wakes, and memorial services provide family members, friends, and loved ones an opportunity to gather together to celebrate the life of the deceased, share stories, offer prayers, and support one another. These ceremonies often reflect the cultural or religious practices of the family, whether through specific rites, songs, prayers, or readings. For many, these rituals provide an essential outlet for grief and a means of affirming the bonds they shared with the person who has passed away. The funeral service can also serve as a communal act of saying goodbye, where mourners come together in solidarity to offer their respects and affirm the life that was lived.

Personal Rituals

Besides funerals, family and loved ones may partake in numerous personal rites to bid farewell. These may encompass the signing of a condolence register, the creation of remembrance albums, or the conduct of private rites or rituals that possess particular significance for the individual or family. Some families may convene to reminisce about cherished memories of the departed, or they may establish a routine of lighting candles or setting a crucifix or flowers at a meaningful location. These commemorative activities might offer solace and assist the bereaved in attaining a sense of tranquility. Establishing personal rituals or activities that commemorate the departed enables family members to sustain a connection with their loved ones and their legacy, even in their absence.

Living Wakes or Celebration of Life

For families and loved ones who are experiencing anticipatory grief, such as when a loved one is terminally ill, saying goodbye can be a long and gradual process, allowing for specific rituals to help prepare for the eventual loss. In this context, families may choose to have "living wakes," which some cultures call "celebrations of life," where they gather with other invitees to offer their love and support while the person is still alive. These gatherings can be deeply meaningful, as they allow family members to express their love, reminisce about memories, and make peace with the inevitable separation. It can also be a time for the individual to share their final wishes, offer their goodbyes, and find comfort in the presence of loved ones before death arrives. Rituals like these are strong healing tools, as they allow everyone to start processing their grief before the loss.

Prayer Vigils and Blessings

Cultural and religious practices also offer a range of specific rituals for saying goodbye. For example, in many religious traditions, rituals such as prayer vigils and blessings offer comfort and help guide individuals through the final moments of life. In the Catholic tradition, rituals like the anointing of the sick can provide spiritual solace as individuals prepare for death. Similarly, in Jewish tradition, the practice of sitting shiva provides an important structure for mourning and commemorating the deceased. These culturally and spiritually grounded rituals not only offer comfort to the dying person but also provide a sense of continuity, reinforcing the belief in a larger spiritual narrative and offering solace to grieving loved ones.

Honoring the Connection to the Body

For many, creating a space for saying goodbye also involves honoring the connection to the body. Rituals such as holding the deceased's hand, speaking to them, or performing last acts of care, such as grooming or arranging their belongings, help individuals feel a sense of closure. Many view the body as a sacred vessel, and these rituals serve as a means of expressing love and respect for it. Touching, holding, and tending to the body in these final moments can also be an important form of emotional expression, as it allows family members to release their grief and process the complex emotions that arise in the moments leading up to and after death.

Spending Quiet Time Together

In addition to the practical and formal rituals, everyday practices for saying goodbye can also be a significant source of comfort. For some, saying goodbye may include simply spending quiet time together, offering a final hug, kiss, or words of affirmation, or doing something meaningful, such as revisiting a favorite place or sharing a special meal. These informal rituals allow families to express love and create lasting memories in their final moments together, without the need for elaborate ceremonies or formalities. The importance of these simple acts cannot be overstated, as they are often the moments that leave an everlasting mark on the hearts of those involved.

Farewells are not solely defined by death; they are intricately interwoven into the essence of life, providing moments for reflection, expression of affection, and the pursuit of tranquility. Through elaborate ceremonies, personal rituals, or subtle acts of compassion, these farewell rituals assist individuals and families in traversing the intricate landscape of grief, memory, and affection. They enable individuals to address the anguish of separation while commemorating the life lived, promoting a sense of tranquility, continuity, and connection that surpasses death. This profoundly human experience is influenced by individual beliefs, cultural traditions, and spiritual ideals, yet it universally offers a venue for healing and closure. Through these rituals, families can initiate healing, recognizing that the love and connection they had will persist, even as they confront the sad reality of farewell.

Other Practical Ways of Saying Goodbye

Other practical ways of saying goodbye include:

1. **Creating Space for Goodbye:** This includes:
    - Acknowledging and expressing grief.
    - Inviting close family and friends to be present.
    - Ensuring the environment is calm and respectful.

    Silence, soft lighting, or playing meaningful music can create a soothing atmosphere conducive to meaningful interaction. Presence often speaks louder than words.

2. **The Power of Words (Final Conversations):** When possible, final conversations are deeply valuable. They often focus on four core messages, outlined by Dr. Ira Byock:
    - "I forgive you."
    - "Please forgive me."

- "Thank you."
- "I love you."[8]

These simple phrases can resolve years of unspoken tension or affirm deep bonds. Even in silence or unconsciousness, talking to the dying person can provide emotional relief and closeness.

3. **Comfort Through Touch:** Touch remains a vital human connector, especially when words are no longer possible. Holding hands, stroking the arm, or gently brushing hair can offer reassurance and communicate love nonverbally. Touch is often used to:
   - Provide grounding and reduce fear.
   - Offer comfort during physical pain.
   - Maintain dignity in the dying process.[9]

4. **Christian Farewells:** In Christian traditions, rituals at the deathbed may include:
   - Reading Scripture (e.g., Ps 23 or John 14).
   - Offering prayers of release and thanksgiving.
   - Administering sacraments such as Anointing of the Sick and Viaticum (final Communion).[10]

   These rituals aim to bring peace, forgiveness, and hope in eternal life.

5. **Islamic Practices:** Muslims often recite the *Shahada*, "There is no god but Allah, and Muhammad is the messenger of Allah," with or for the dying person. Friends and family may:
   - Sit quietly and pray.
   - Read Surah Yasin aloud.
   - Help position the body to face Mecca.[11]

   Maintaining calm and dignity is central in Islamic end-of-life rites.

8. Byock, *Four Things That Matter*, 3.
9. Ferrell and Coyle, *Oxford Textbook of Palliative Nursing*, 410–12.
10. United States Conference of Catholic Bishops, *Pastoral Care*, 29–31.
11. Gatrad and Sheikh, "Palliative Care for Muslims," 594.

6. **Buddhist Farewells:** In Buddhism, death is seen as a crucial moment for spiritual liberation. Practices may include:

    - Chanting the name of the Buddha (e.g., Amitabha).
    - Creating a peaceful atmosphere free of distractions.
    - Meditating on compassion and letting go of attachments.[12]

    For Tibetan Buddhists, readings from the Tibetan Book of the Dead help guide the consciousness during transition.

7. **Indigenous Traditions:** Many Native American and Indigenous communities have practices that involve:

    - Singing spiritual songs.
    - Smudging with sage or cedar to purify the space.
    - Storytelling to honor the dying person's life and ancestors.[13]

    These rites help both the individual and community make peace with death.

8. **Secular and Personalized Rituals:** Not all goodbyes are religious. Personal rituals may include:

    - Creating a memory circle where loved ones share stories.
    - Playing the dying person's favorite music.
    - Lighting candles or writing farewell letters.

    Legacy projects such as photo albums, audio recordings, or art-making provide a tangible way to preserve memories.[14]

9. **Saying What Was Left Unsaid:** The process of dying often brings unresolved issues to the surface. Saying goodbye can include:

    - Apologies or words of reconciliation.
    - Sharing final wishes.
    - Asking for guidance or offering blessings.

12. Singh, *Grace in Dying*, 74–78.
13. Brown, *Sacred Pipe*, 91–94.
14. Remen, *My Grandfather's Blessings*, 213–18.

Even in complicated relationships, this time can be transformative, allowing space for healing or letting go.

10. **Accepting the Transition:** When death feels near, caregivers can gently speak words like "It's OK to go" or "You can rest now." These affirmations support the dying person in releasing fear or attachment. Hospice nurses and chaplains often guide families in this kind of farewell.[15]

Conclusively, to say goodbye to a dying person is an act of profound intimacy and courage. Whether shaped by faith, culture, or personal meaning, these rituals create a sacred space for connection, love, and acceptance. In honoring the dying process, we affirm life itself and the enduring bonds of the human spirit.

15. Callanan and Kelley, *Final Gifts*, 36–39.

7

The Companioned Path

(Grief Care in Christian Ministry)

STORY 1: THE EMPTY CHAIR

In the small town of Compton, Illinois, lived a kindhearted pastor named Grace. She was known not just for her sermons, but for the way she listened, truly listened, with her whole being. Her office, tucked behind the old chapel, had become a haven for those whose hearts were heavy.

One rainy afternoon, a young woman named Isabel came to see her. Her eyes were red-rimmed, her shoulders hunched as if carrying the weight of a mountain. In her hand, she clutched a worn photograph of a little girl with braided hair and a dimpled smile.

"She was my sister," she whispered. "Lila. We lost her last month. It doesn't feel real."

Pastor Grace gestured to a chair beside her desk, one she kept intentionally empty.

"Would you like to tell me about her?" she asked gently.

As Isabel spoke, something happened. The rawness in her voice softened. She spoke of tea parties with plastic cups, the way Lila laughed at her own jokes, how she would sneak into her room during thunderstorms. Each memory painted her not just as gone, but as someone who had been, vividly, fully, beautifully.

Pastor Grace didn't rush to explain, or try to fix what was broken. She simply held the space, sacred and still, for Isabel's grief.

"You know," she said after a while, "that empty chair, it's always there for the ones we've lost. Sometimes we need to talk to them, or about them, or just sit quietly in their absence."

Isabel looked at the chair, now filled with a presence only her heart could sense. "I think she would've liked that."

Over the months, Isabel kept coming back. Sometimes she cried, sometimes she just sat in silence. Through her grief, she learned to see that mourning wasn't about "moving on" but about "moving forward," carrying Lila with her, not leaving her behind.

Over time, Isabel began helping others at the chapel, becoming a quiet companion for those starting their own journeys through loss.

Reflection: *Grief counseling and pastoral care are not about having all the answers. They're about being present when no answer feels good enough. They're about sitting beside someone in their pain, reminding them they are not alone, and honoring the love that loss can never erase.*

Just like the empty chair in Pastor Grace's office, grief creates space in our hearts, not just for sorrow, but eventually, for hope.

Grief is a universal human experience, yet each individual's journey through loss is deeply personal. Whether the loss is due to death, separation, or other significant life changes, the emotional and spiritual impact can be overwhelming. Grief counseling and spiritual care play pivotal roles in providing support, comfort, and healing for individuals navigating the complexities of loss. These two forms of care, while distinct in their approaches, work in tandem to address the psychological, emotional, and spiritual dimensions of grief. Both aim to help individuals process their pain, make sense of their loss, and identify pathways toward healing and hope.

UNDERSTANDING THE PSYCHOLOGICAL AND EMOTIONAL JOURNEY IN GRIEF COUNSELING

Grief counseling is a therapeutic approach that focuses on helping individuals understand and cope with the psychological and emotional responses that arise from loss. Professional grief counselors are trained to provide a safe space where individuals can express their feelings, explore the many facets of their grief, and develop coping strategies. Grief counseling can be offered individually, in groups, or through family therapy, depending on the needs of the person or family experiencing loss. The role of a grief counselor is not to "fix" the grief but to support the individual in navigating their emotions and finding healthy ways to cope.

One of the foundational elements of grief counseling is the acknowledgment that there is no "right" or "wrong" way to grieve. Grief manifests differently for each person, influenced by the nature of the loss, the relationship to the deceased, cultural factors, and individual coping mechanisms. A skilled grief counselor helps individuals understand the different emotional responses to grief, which may include sadness, anger, guilt, confusion, or even numbness. Counselors may use various therapeutic techniques, such as cognitive behavioral therapy (CBT), narrative therapy, or art and music therapy, to help individuals express their grief and reframe their thoughts about the loss.

An important aspect of grief counseling is addressing the physical and psychological symptoms of grief. Many individuals experience physical discomfort, such as fatigue, headaches, or difficulty sleeping, as a result of their grief. When individuals identify these symptoms, normalize them as part of the grieving process, and explore strategies for self-care and stress management, healing begins to manifest. There is a need to also understand the concept of "complicated grief," where the mourning process becomes prolonged or hindered due to unresolved emotions, trauma, or other psychological factors. In such cases, grief counseling can help individuals process and work through their emotions, providing them with the tools to eventually find healing.

Providing Pastoral Care and Comfort

Pastoral care, on the other hand, focuses on providing spiritual and emotional support from a faith-based perspective. It is grounded in the belief that spirituality plays an integral role in helping individuals attain meaning, comfort, and hope in the face of suffering and loss. Pastoral care is typically offered by religious leaders, chaplains, or spiritual counselors who are trained to support individuals within the framework of their faith tradition. In times of grief, pastoral care provides a sense of connection to something larger than oneself, whether that be God, a higher power, or a community of faith.

The role of the pastoral caregiver is multifaceted. First and foremost, pastoral care offers a compassionate presence for those who are grieving. Often, the grieving process can feel isolating, and individuals may discover it is difficult to articulate their pain or doubts. A pastor or chaplain provides a listening ear and emotional support, affirming the person's feelings while offering comfort through prayer, scripture, or spiritual guidance. In this way, pastoral care offers a sense of solidarity, reminding individuals that they are not alone in their suffering.

A crucial aspect of care is helping individuals discover meaning in their grief. At such moments, mourners are encouraged to explore existential questions about life, death, and the afterlife, using the teachings of their faith tradition to provide solace and understanding. For example, many Christian traditions emphasize the hope of resurrection and eternal life, which can provide a deep sense of peace to those grieving the loss of a loved one. In other faith traditions, the understanding of reincarnation, karma, or the continuity of the soul can offer similar comfort. By helping individuals explore the spiritual dimensions of their grief, pastoral care encourages hope, healing, and a sense of purpose beyond the immediate pain of loss.

INTEGRATING GRIEF COUNSELING AND PASTORAL CARE

(A Holistic Approach)

While grief counseling and pastoral care have distinct roles, they are often most effective when integrated. A holistic approach to grief care addresses the psychological, emotional, and spiritual needs of the individual. Following a loss, many individuals experience both emotional distress and spiritual questioning, and it is impossible to neatly separate these experiences. For example, a person may experience feelings of guilt or anger, and these emotions may not only stem from their personal history but also from spiritual doubts or questions about the afterlife. By combining the compassionate listening and therapeutic techniques of grief counseling with the spiritual guidance and rituals of pastoral care, families and individuals can receive comprehensive support that addresses their whole being.

Collaboration between grief counselors and spiritual caregivers can also help provide continuity of care. In some cases, a grieving person may begin with grief counseling and later seek pastoral support as they process their grief from a more spiritual or existential perspective. Conversely, some individuals may initially turn to their pastor or spiritual advisor and later seek counseling when they determine that their emotional distress requires more in-depth psychological support. A coordinated approach ensures that both the emotional and spiritual aspects of grief are addressed and that individuals have access to the full range of resources available.

GRIEF AND GUILT

Grief and guilt often intertwine in the aftermath of loss, compounding emotional distress for those who mourn. While grief is a natural response to losing a loved one, guilt can stem from unresolved conflicts, perceived failures, or survival itself. This combination may manifest as persistent thoughts, emotional numbness, or self-blame, potentially impeding the healing process. According to Worden, addressing these complex emotions is crucial for adapting to loss and progressing through mourning tasks.[1] Without appropriate coping mechanisms, unresolved guilt can lead to prolonged or complicated grief.

Effective coping strategies include cognitive reframing, where individuals challenge irrational beliefs about their role in the loss, and expressive therapies such as journaling or art, which facilitate emotional processing. Professional interventions, like grief counseling or cognitive behavioral therapy (CBT), may also be essential in helping individuals disentangle guilt from grief.[2] Support groups can provide communal validation, normalizing the grieving experience and alleviating the isolating effects of guilt.

1. Worden, *Grief Counseling and Grief Therapy*, 62.
2. Shear, "Complicated Grief," 153–60.

Ultimately, understanding that grief and guilt are natural, though painful, responses can empower individuals to seek help and practice self-compassion. Mental health professionals emphasize that guilt feelings, however intense, often reflect the depth of one's connection to the deceased rather than objective failings.[3] Healing from loss involves not just accepting absence but also integrating memories and reshaping life narratives. Through compassionate support and evidence-based interventions, those burdened by guilt can gradually find meaning and peace in their grief journey.

Story 2: The Weight of Grief

Elaine never wanted children of her own. But when her younger brother, Mark, won custody of his five-year-old son, Liam, after a bitter divorce, she stepped in without hesitation. Mark worked long hours as an air traffic controller, and Elaine, single, steady, and reliable, became the boy's second mother. She cooked his meals, read him bedtime stories, and whispered promises that she'd always keep him safe.

But one warm July afternoon shattered that promise.

There were an accident and Liam died on the spot.

In the weeks that followed, Elaine couldn't speak without trembling. Her brother, hollow-eyed and broken, didn't blame her aloud. He didn't have to. She blamed herself enough for both of them. She stopped seeing friends. Stopped answering calls. Sundays, which once meant pancakes and cartoons with Liam, became unbearable. She stopped going to church entirely. "God took him," she told herself. "Or worse, God watched, and did nothing."

Many years passed; she never married, never celebrated her birthday. Every child's laughter became a dagger to the heart. She worked in silence, lived in silence, aged in silence. She refused therapy, convinced she didn't deserve healing. Each night, she whispered to Liam's photo, "I'm sorry, baby. I'm sorry."

Her life changed when her body failed her, as a sudden cardiac episode led to hospitalization and forced her to slow down. While on her hospital bed, a chaplain visited. Elaine wanted to refuse her. But the chaplain didn't offer prayers right away. Instead, she sat quietly. Then she asked gently, "Who have you lost?"

The question undid Elaine.

3. Worden, *Grief Counseling and Grief Therapy*, 87.

For the first time in years, she told the whole story. Not just the death, but the suffocating years that followed. She wept until she couldn't speak.

The chaplain said something simple: "God grieved that day too."

Elaine shook her head, disbelieving.

Chaplain continued softly, "Punishing yourself won't bring Liam back. But letting go of the guilt doesn't mean you've forgotten him. It means you're letting love speak louder than blame."

Elaine didn't accept those words immediately. Healing wasn't a miracle. It was a process. Over weeks, then months, she allowed herself small mercies: walking outside without guilt, visiting Liam's grave without apology, telling Mark the truth, that she still woke from nightmares.

In time, she lit a candle in church, not for forgiveness, but as a sign that she was ready to remember Liam's life, not just his death.

She would carry grief always. But at last, the weight of guilt began to lift.

Not forgotten. Not erased.

But finally forgiven.

Story 3: Anna's Missed Warning

Anna was twenty-nine when her younger sister, Grace, died by suicide. In the months leading up to it, Anna remembered texts that seemed "off" but dismissed them as mood swings. The night before Grace died, Anna ignored a call, thinking, "I'll call her tomorrow." Tomorrow never came. For years, Anna's grief was tangled with brutal guilt. She withdrew from friends, couldn't enter Grace's bedroom at their parents' house, and silently replayed every conversation, convinced she could've saved her.

Therapy felt impossible at first. "Talking won't bring her back," Anna told herself. But five years later, after a panic attack left her hospitalized, she finally saw a grief counselor. Her therapist helped her understand that suicide is never the fault of one missed text or ignored call. Healing wasn't quick, but over months, Anna learned to differentiate her love from her responsibility. She created a scrapbook of Grace's life, not focused on her death, but on her living moments. Slowly, Anna forgave herself, not all at once, but enough to start living again.

Story 4: James and the Red Light

James had been driving the night his wife, Mia, was killed. They'd argued earlier, and during the drive, he ran a red light, distracted. A drunk driver hit them. James survived; Mia didn't. "If only I'd stopped at that light . . ." was the sentence that consumed him for years. He avoided the intersection, stopped driving altogether, and pushed friends away, convinced he didn't deserve forgiveness.

Ten years passed. The grief hardened into a quiet emptiness. At a memorial Mass for road accident victims at St. Mary of the Lake Church, James met a man who had also lost someone. They talked for hours, not about blame, but about pain. Encouraged, James sought therapy, but what changed him most was volunteering for a road safety awareness campaign. He told his story, not to punish himself, but to prevent others from sharing it. In speaking publicly, he found a strange peace: Mia wouldn't want him to carry this burden alone. One day, trembling, he drove through that fateful intersection. It was the hardest thing he had done. But as the light turned green, he felt something loosen inside, a permission to keep moving forward.

Story 5: Rosa's Forgotten Appointment

Rosa's father died of a heart attack one morning. She had promised to take him to the doctor. Unfortunately, she overslept. He was gone when she arrived. For twenty years, Rosa believed she had killed him through negligence. Life moved on, marriage, children, but the guilt never left. Every Father's Day, she avoided the cemetery, too ashamed to visit.

Her healing began not through therapy, but by accident. Her daughter, age sixteen, missed an important event and was inconsolable, sobbing, "I ruined everything." Holding her child, Rosa said, "Mistakes don't make you bad." Saying those words cracked something in herself. Could she forgive herself for one mistake made as a tired, overworked daughter? She began journaling, then eventually saw a grief counselor, who helped her understand that her father's health had been failing long before that morning. His death wasn't on her shoulders alone.

In time, Rosa visited her father's grave. She didn't apologize. She talked about her life, her kids, and her guilt, and then, she said goodbye to that guilt. Not perfectly, but honestly. Every Father's Day since, she's brought flowers, not shame.

THE INDIVIDUAL DEALING WITH GRIEF

Grief, in its rawest form, is an overwhelming tide of emotions that can leave one feeling disoriented and broken. In these moments, one of the most essential ways to cope is by allowing oneself to fully feel the pain rather than suppressing it. Pretending to be strong can create deeper wounds over time. Instead, embracing the sadness, anger, confusion, or even numbness as valid parts of the grieving process allows healing to begin. Whether through tears, solitude, writing, or prayer, expressing those emotions becomes a way of honoring the depth of the loss and the love behind it.

Supportive relationships can be a crucial source of strength during this emotional turmoil. Grief often feels like an isolating experience, but having someone to talk to, such as a friend, family member, spiritual leader, or counselor, can make a significant difference. Occasionally, what helps most is not advice, but simply the comforting presence of someone willing to listen and share the burden. Community support, whether through shared faith, grief groups, or trusted companions, reminds us that we are not alone. In shared stories and compassionate silence, we begin to see that healing is possible, even if the pain does not completely disappear.

Identifying minor rituals and sources of purpose can gradually restore a sense of stability to daily living. Ordinary activities such as walking, cooking, or pursuing hobbies may appear trivial, yet they re-instill a sense of normalcy and agency amidst chaos. For numerous individuals, seeking solace in faith following bereavement can yield profound consolation, presenting the promise of spiritual solace, everlasting life, or heavenly friendship amid adversity. Faith frequently serves as a source of hope and resilience, whether expressed through Scripture, liturgy, or periods of peaceful contemplation. As days go into weeks and months, sadness progressively transforms. While the loss persists within you, so does the strength you uncover, the support you obtain, and the subtle ways in which life commences to flourish anew.

PROVIDING ONGOING SUPPORT TO THE BEREAVED

Story 6: The Garden of Hope

There lived a woman named Joy, known by neighbors for her vibrant laughter and sun-drenched garden that bloomed brighter than any other for miles.

Her roses, she often said, taught her more about life than any book ever could, especially about beginnings, endings, and the miracles of life.

Joy lived with her husband Tom and their son Mika, whose love was woven into the very soil they tended. Their family was a happy one, until one day, a storm swept the town. It wasn't the thunder or wind that shattered Joy's world, but the silence that followed. Tom and Mika, caught in a road mishap during the storm, never came home.

The town mourned with Joy, but grief is a house with many locked rooms. For months, Joy wandered her home like a ghost. Her garden, once bursting with color, grew wild and brittle. Neighbors whispered of her fading spirit, how even her laughter had been taken by the sea.

One bright morning, an old woman arrived in town and wandered to Joy's garden. She was a mystery, carrying nothing but a canvas bag of seeds and eyes that held whole histories. She found Joy sitting motionless on her porch and said, simply, "I lost my son, too. Years ago."

Joy looked up, not to speak but to listen, because something in the woman's presence felt like the first sun after a long, unkind, cloudy weather.

The woman continued, "After he was buried, I didn't speak for two years. I stopped cooking, stopped singing, even stopped praying. Then one day, a child from the village came to my door with a cracked pot and said, 'Can you teach me to grow joy again?' I couldn't say no."

She opened her bag and pulled out a single blue cornflower seed. "I learned that loss never leaves us, but it can teach us to plant things again. This seed is for you, not for your garden, but for your spirit."

That evening, Joy planted the seed.

She didn't expect much. But she watered it. And when it sprouted, she planted another. The garden slowly responded, not because it needed tending, but because Joy needed something to care for again. She started writing letters to Tom and Mika, placing them in glass jars among the flower beds. She read them aloud at dusk, letting the wind carry her words.

One evening, a little came to Joy and whispered, "This place feels like it remembers how to smile."

Years passed. The garden bloomed wildly once more, but not as it had before. It had scars, bent branches, odd shadows, wild thorns among the roses. It was beautiful because it was honest. So was Joy.

Reflection: *Loss carves out space for a deeper kind of strength. Resilience doesn't mean never breaking; it means letting yourself bloom again in broken places. And hope, like a garden, needs light, patience, and the courage to believe that something beautiful can still rise.*

The journey of grief does not end after the funeral or memorial service; in fact, for many individuals, the real work of mourning begins in the days, weeks, and even months following the loss. Providing ongoing support to the bereaved is crucial in helping them navigate this often long and difficult process. Grief is not something that can be "fixed" quickly, and there is no specific timeline for healing. Instead, the bereaved need continued care, understanding, and encouragement as they adjust to life without their loved one. Ongoing support addresses the evolving needs of individuals as they cope with the emotional, psychological, and practical challenges that arise during their grieving journey.

One of the most important aspects of ongoing support is maintaining a connection with the bereaved after the initial period of mourning. Often, after the funeral and memorial service, friends and family may return to their regular lives, which can leave the grieving person feeling isolated and abandoned. It is essential for caregivers, counselors, spiritual leaders, and loved ones to reach out and speak with the bereaved in the weeks and months following the loss. Simple acts of care, such as phone calls, text messages, or invitations to lunch, can provide a sense of connection and remind the person that they are not alone. These interactions can play a crucial role in shielding the bereaved from feelings of isolation or neglecting their grief.

For many, the bereavement process extends beyond the immediate sadness of loss and includes the gradual process of adjusting to a new reality. As time passes, the bereaved often experience a range of emotions: anger, guilt, regret, confusion, and sometimes even relief. These emotions can fluctuate, and the grieving person may face moments when they feel as though they are "moving forward" only to be struck by intense feelings of loss once again. It's vital to know that grieving is a process with no "right" way to do it. Thus, one is encouraged to be patient with oneself and avoid self-judgment, as many people feel pressure to "move on" quickly, which can complicate their emotional healing.

Another key component of ongoing support is providing opportunities for the bereaved to share their feelings and experiences. Grief can often feel like an internalized experience, where individuals struggle to articulate their pain or fear of being a burden to others. Creating safe spaces where the bereaved can express their emotions without fear of judgment or dismissal is vital. Support groups, therapy, or even informal gatherings with close friends can provide the bereaved with opportunities to speak openly about their grief. Connecting with others who are experiencing similar emotions can also offer a sense of solidarity and understanding that can help the grieving person feel seen and heard.

Practical support also plays a crucial role in ongoing care. The period of bereavement can be overwhelming, especially when it involves managing day-to-day tasks that may have previously been shared with the deceased. This can include everything from household chores and financial matters to decision-making around the deceased's belongings. Offering practical help, whether through meal preparation, assistance with organizing the deceased's estate, or helping with childcare or errands, can relieve some of the burdens the bereaved are facing. By providing this tangible support, caregivers can ease the practical strain, allowing the grieving person to focus on their emotional wellbeing and processing their grief.

In addition to emotional and practical support, it is important to acknowledge and support the bereaved in their search for meaning. The process of grieving often leads people to question aspects of their identity, their faith, or their understanding of life and death. Many people turn to their spirituality to help make sense of their loss, seeking comfort through prayer, meditation, or religious practices. Guiding individuals through this spiritual exploration is of the essence. Helping individuals locate ways to honor their loved ones and maintain relationships with them even after death is an important aspect of healing.

Understanding the long-term effects of grief is another aspect of ongoing support. As time passes, the bereaved may experience new challenges in their grief journey, such as anniversaries, holidays, or significant life events that highlight their loss. These "trigger" moments can often bring the pain of loss back to the forefront, and the grieving person may feel like they are reexperiencing their grief all over again. Awareness of these difficult times can help the individual to deal with them in a more positive way, maybe by simply acknowledging the struggle or seeking additional help and feeling less alone in their journey.

Furthermore, it is essential to recognize that grief is not a linear process, and healing does not mean forgetting the loved one. Rather, healing involves finding ways to live with the loss and integrate it into one's life in a way that allows for growth and eventual peace. Ongoing support should emphasize the importance of self-compassion, resilience, and personal growth. Encouraging the bereaved to seek professional help when needed, whether through individual counseling or group therapy, can ensure that they continue to receive the emotional support necessary to process their grief in a healthy manner. As the grieving person moves through their journey, they may begin to find ways to honor the memory of their loved one.

ADDRESSING COMPLICATED OR PROLONGED GRIEF

Grief is a deeply personal and complex experience, and while most individuals will eventually find a way to adjust to their loss, some may struggle with complicated or prolonged grief. Unlike the natural, gradual healing that occurs with typical bereavement, complicated grief is characterized by intense, persistent symptoms that significantly impair one's ability to function. This form of grief can be prolonged, lasting months or even years, and is often marked by an overwhelming sense of longing or yearning for the deceased, difficulty accepting the reality of the loss, or an inability to engage in life without the person who has died. Addressing complicated or prolonged grief requires a thoughtful, multifaceted approach that combines emotional support, therapeutic intervention, and practical guidance.

Understanding Complicated Grief

People with complicated grief may experience intense and chronic feelings of sorrow, bitterness, or anger, and they may feel that they cannot move forward in life after their loved one's death. Common symptoms of complicated grief include intrusive thoughts or images of the deceased, constant feelings of disbelief or denial about the loss, difficulty trusting others or engaging in relationships, and a profound sense of meaninglessness or lack of purpose. These symptoms can interfere with daily functioning and lead to significant emotional and psychological distress, including depression, anxiety, and even suicidal ideation.

In addition to emotional symptoms, complicated grief may manifest in physical ways, such as sleep disturbances, fatigue, and loss of appetite. People suffering from complicated grief may also engage in maladaptive coping strategies, such as substance abuse or isolation, as they attempt to avoid or numb their overwhelming emotions. The intensity and persistence of these feelings can make it challenging for individuals to process their grief and begin to heal. Understanding that complicated grief is a legitimate and distressing condition is essential for offering appropriate care and support.

Approaching Complicated Grief with Compassion

The initial step in confronting complicated grief is to engage with profound empathy and comprehension. Individuals experiencing complicated sorrow may perceive themselves as "stuck" in the mourning process and may experience guilt or shame for their inability to progress. They may experience a sense of disconnection from individuals who seem to be recovering more rapidly, or they may perceive that their sadness diminishes the memories of their loved ones. It is essential for caretakers, counselors, and loved ones to establish a secure, nonjudgmental environment in which the bereaved can articulate their emotions without the apprehension of being advised to "move on" or "get over it." Engaging in active listening and providing validation significantly aids in making the individual feel comprehended and supported during periods of overwhelming grief and isolation.

Recognizing that complicated grief is not a sign of weakness or failure is crucial for both the grieving individual and those providing support. Rather than expecting the person to "snap out of it" or "get back to normal," it is important to acknowledge that healing from a significant loss is often a gradual and nonlinear process. Individuals experiencing complicated grief may need more time, space, and assistance to work through their emotions and come to terms with their loss. Providing ongoing, compassionate support allows individuals to feel that they are not alone in their journey and that there is hope for healing, even if it seems far off.

Therapeutic Interventions for Complicated Grief

For individuals struggling with complicated grief, therapeutic intervention may be necessary to help them process their emotions and begin to heal. Grief counseling and psychotherapy can offer valuable tools and strategies for managing the intense emotions and thoughts associated with complicated grief. Cognitive behavioral therapy (CBT) has been found to be especially effective for complicated grief, as it helps individuals identify and challenge negative thought patterns that may be perpetuating their distress. In particular, CBT can assist individuals in reframing their thoughts about the loss and developing healthier coping mechanisms for dealing with intrusive memories, rumination, or feelings of guilt.[4] In addition, evidence-based approaches such as complicated grief treatment (CGT), which integrates elements of CBT with interpersonal therapy, have demonstrated significant efficacy in reducing symptoms and promoting adaptive mourning.[5] Structured support from trained therapists is therefore critical in addressing the unique challenges faced by individuals experiencing complicated grief.

Another therapeutic approach that has shown promise in treating complicated grief is prolonged exposure therapy (PET). This approach involves gradually confronting and processing memories and emotions related to the loss in a controlled and supportive manner. Through this process, individuals can learn to tolerate the painful emotions associated with grief and ultimately reduce the distress they cause. Eye movement desensitization and reprocessing (EMDR) therapy has also been used successfully for complicated grief, as it helps individuals process traumatic memories of loss by using bilateral stimulation to facilitate emotional processing.[6]

In some cases, medication may be prescribed to help manage symptoms of complicated grief, particularly if the individual is experiencing depression, anxiety, or other mental health conditions that complicate their grieving process. Antidepressants or anti-anxiety medications may be recommended by a healthcare provider to alleviate some of the emotional symptoms that prevent the person from functioning or processing their grief. Always consider medication as part of a comprehensive treatment plan and use it in conjunction with therapy to provide holistic support.

Spiritual and Community Support

In addition to formal therapeutic interventions, spiritual care and community support can play an essential role in addressing complicated grief. Many individuals experiencing prolonged grief may find themselves questioning their faith or grappling with existential questions about life, death, and the afterlife. For those who are religious or spiritual, turning to their faith for support can provide comfort, meaning, and a sense of connection to a higher power. Pastoral care, spiritual counseling, and religious

4. Shear, "Complicated Grief," 153–60.
5. Simon et al., "Complicated Grief," 617–23.
6. Simon et al., "Diagnosis and Treatment," 736–47.

rituals such as prayer, meditation, or remembrance ceremonies can offer a framework for understanding the loss and finding hope amidst suffering. Religious communities can also provide a network of support, offering opportunities for the grieving person to feel part of a caring, compassionate group of people who can walk alongside them in their journey.

Fostering Meaning and Acceptance

In navigating complicated grief, a crucial aspect of healing entails cultivating purpose and acceptance. It is crucial to recognize the profound feelings associated with loss while also assisting the bereaved in assimilating their grief into their life to discover renewed meaning and direction. This may entail discovering methods to commemorate the deceased, including establishing a memorial, participating in philanthropic endeavors in their honor, or adopting a new routine that preserves the remembrance of the loved one in significant ways. Engaging in activities that provide joy, significance, or fulfillment might facilitate a transition from profound melancholy to a more balanced perspective.

It is important to emphasize that healing from complicated grief does not mean forgetting or "moving on" from the loss. Instead, healing involves finding a way to live with the loss, to integrate the memory of the loved one, and to move forward with life while carrying the grief. This journey may take time, but with the right support, therapy, and community care, it is possible to attain healing, peace, and renewed purpose.

Summarily, addressing complicated or prolonged grief is a vital part of the grieving process. Understanding the unique challenges that individuals face when their grief becomes complicated or prolonged is crucial. Caregivers, therapists, and spiritual leaders can offer targeted support to help these individuals process their emotions, build resilience, and find healing. Therapeutic interventions, spiritual care, community support, and the development of new meaning are essential components in helping the bereaved move forward in a healthy way. With time, compassion, and the right resources, individuals can begin to navigate the depths of their grief, heal, and learn to live fully again, even in the presence of loss.

BUILDING RESILIENCE AND NURTURING HOPE AFTER LOSS

The experience of loss is one of life's most challenging and transformative events. Whether it is the death of a loved one, the end of a relationship, or the loss of health or opportunity, grief can leave a deep emotional and psychological imprint. However, while the pain of loss can be profound, it is possible to build resilience and nurture hope in the aftermath. Resilience is the ability to adapt to difficult circumstances, bounce back from adversity, and continue moving forward, even when life seems overwhelming. Nurturing hope is the process of cultivating a sense of possibility and meaning despite suffering, and it plays a crucial role in the healing journey. By fostering resilience and hope, individuals can experience strength, growth, and renewal in the wake of loss.

Story 7: How to Begin Again

A woman named Norah, in her fifties with eyes that had known too many goodbyes, began coming to a community square every Sunday to relax, take some fresh air, and listen to nature. She brought a journal and a flask of tea to sip from. She would always leave a small note tucked under the bench at the square. The notes were simple:

"Breathe. The sun rose again today."

"You are not your worst day."

"Grief is proof that you dared to love deeply."

Gradually, the bench became a quiet gathering spot for people who had loved and lost. Some came to weep, others to think, and a few came just to sit, unsure of what else to do.

Soon, people started noticing. One by one, others began leaving their own notes, folded, scrawled, sometimes tear-stained:

"Today I miss her. But I also smiled at a memory."

"I got out of bed. That's enough for now."

"He would've wanted me to keep painting."

Soon, a small box was attached under the bench with a sign: "For your grief. For your growth."

And the community square became more than a resting place. It became a garden of resilience, quiet, collective, and sacred.

Norah never signed her name. But one day, a young man in a hoodie sat beside her and said, "I lost my brother. I thought I was broken until I read one of your notes."

Norah smiled gently and replied, "You're not broken. You're breaking open."

Reflection: *Grief is not a sign of weakness; it's the echo of love. And resilience isn't about bouncing back to who you were; it's about growing into who you can be. When we share our sorrow and sow our hope, we discover that healing is not an individual journey; it's a human one.*

Understanding Resilience in the Grieving Process

Resilience is not about avoiding pain or "getting over" grief quickly. Rather, it involves the capacity to face the pain, experience it fully, and continue to live and engage with the world despite it. Grief can alter a person's identity, perspective, and way of interacting with others. However, resilience allows individuals to process their emotions in a healthy way, learn from their experiences, and eventually find a new equilibrium. Resilience does not mean that the person forgets their loss, but that they develop the inner strength to integrate it into their life in a way that allows them to continue living meaningfully.

There are several key factors that contribute to resilience after loss. One of the most important is the presence of social support. Having a network of caring friends, family members, or support groups can provide emotional comfort, reduce feelings of isolation, and help individuals navigate the difficult moments of grief. Social support allows individuals to feel seen and understood in their pain, which creates an emotional bond that helps them rebuild their sense of self and belonging in the world.

Another essential factor in building resilience is the ability to maintain a sense of routine and stability. While the grief process can cause profound disruption in one's life, maintaining regular activities, such as work, hobbies, physical exercise, or spiritual practices, can help provide a sense of normalcy and purpose. Even small acts of self-care, like getting out of bed, preparing a meal, or taking a walk, can serve as important steps toward resilience by allowing individuals to reclaim their agency and take control of their lives again.

Finding Strength Through Vulnerability

An essential aspect of resilience is allowing oneself to be vulnerable. Many individuals feel the need to suppress their emotions or avoid expressing their pain, believing that grief must be faced privately or that they must "be strong" for others. However, resilience is not about emotional suppression; it's about embracing vulnerability and allowing oneself to feel deeply.[7] It is through acknowledging and expressing grief that individuals can begin to process their emotions and find healing. Vulnerability, whether through talking to a therapist, sharing with a loved one, or participating in support groups, can foster emotional release and create opportunities for personal growth.[8] By embracing vulnerability, individuals also learn to build emotional flexibility.[9] Resilience involves the capacity to adapt and bend with life's difficulties without breaking. While grief may feel overwhelming, embracing vulnerability allows individuals to experience their grief without becoming consumed by it, ultimately finding new pathways toward healing.

Nurturing Hope Through Meaning-Making

Hope is a crucial component in the healing process. It offers a glimmer of hope amidst the darkness and ambiguity of mourning. Spirituality and faith establish a foundation for cultivating hope in numerous individuals. People may find comfort in believing their loved ones live on, whether in the afterlife, reincarnation, or through their impact on the world. Individuals may resort to religious practices such as prayer or meditation to attain peace, comfort, and hope. In this context, spirituality assists individuals in perceiving their grief as a component of a broader narrative, providing a link to a transcendent entity. This conviction in a transcendent purpose or divine scheme can furnish the fortitude required to withstand adversity and cultivate optimism for the future.

Nurturing hope can cultivate optimism, even among individuals who do not adhere to a specific religious tradition. In the context of loss, meaning-making can manifest in several ways, including honoring the departed, pursuing their treasured interests or vocations, or leveraging the loss to enhance one's own existence. Numerous individuals observe that

7. Brown, *Power of Vulnerability*, xx.

8. Bonanno, *Other Side of Sadness*, 75–89.

9. Doka and Tucci, *Living with Grief*, 22–35.

their loss motivates them to pursue opportunities or alternative avenues they may not have previously considered. The outcome may involve engaging in self-improvement endeavors, acquiring new hobbies, or contributing to society through philanthropic initiatives. Individuals may cultivate hope by discovering novel methods to lead meaningful lives as they reassess their sense of purpose after experiencing a loss.

Encouraging Growth Through Grief

Grief can be transformative, leading to personal growth despite the pain. Resilience and hope do not necessarily mean returning to the way life was before the loss, but rather finding new ways to live and thrive despite the changes. Many individuals report that their grief journey ultimately helped them become more empathetic, compassionate, and connected to others. By working through grief, individuals can develop a more profound understanding of themselves, their relationships, and the preciousness of life itself. As part of this process, it is important for the bereaved to recognize their own strengths and the ways they have coped with their grief. Acknowledging the resilience that has allowed them to navigate their pain can help rebuild self-esteem and confidence.

Summarily, building resilience and nurturing hope after loss is an essential part of the healing process. Resilience enables individuals to face grief head-on, allowing them to identify strength in vulnerability, create new meaning, and maintain connection with their loved ones. Hope, in turn, provides a sense of possibility, helping individuals believe that healing is possible even in the darkest of times. Through support, meaning-making, rituals, and personal growth, individuals can move through their grief journey with greater peace, strength, and optimism. While the pain of loss may never fully disappear, resilience and hope allow individuals to integrate their grief into their lives in a way that promotes healing, renewal, and continued growth.

8

Self-Care and Mental Hygiene

(Care for Oneself Leads to Better Care for Others)

STORY: THE TEACUP

There was once a young woman named Lila who was always busy with work, school, social obligations, and endless scrolling. She bragged that she didn't need sleep and that rest was "for the weak." One day, she visited her wise grandmother, who served her tea. But instead of stopping when the cup was full, Grandma kept pouring. Tea spilled everywhere.

"Grandma! Stop! It's overflowing!" Lila voiced out.

Her grandmother smiled gently. "So is your mind, sweetheart. You can't keep pouring things into it without emptying some out."

From that day on, Lila started each morning with ten minutes of silence and a cup of tea to begin the day, and considered rest important for better performance.

Reflection: *Like a teacup, one's mind needs empty space to be useful.*

IN TODAY'S FAST-PACED AND hyper-connected world, taking care of one's overall health has become not just important but essential. Anyone in the ministry of care can only function properly and pay attention to the needs of others if they are able to identify first their personal needs, name their feelings at any given time, and attend to them. While the concepts of self-care and mental hygiene may seem like buzzwords, they are actually grounded in psychological science and represent practical strategies for maintaining emotional balance, reducing stress, and enhancing overall wellbeing.

An Igbo adage says, "He who fights and runs away lives to fight again." This adage can be used to qualify the importance of self-care for the continuity of one's life and that of others. One needs to be alive and healthy to be able to continue in the ministry of care. According to Keith-Spiegel and Koocher, as cited by Wityk, giving of oneself for the sake of others is admirable. However, if one does not balance this giving with self-care, it can lead to burnout, which may result in ethical violations.[1] Thus, to flourish in the ministry of care, there is a need to take care of oneself. Wityk cited Muldary, who states that there is a drop in general motivation to deliver high-quality care when zeal and commitment wane.[2]

UNDERSTANDING SELF-CARE AND MENTAL HYGIENE

Self-care is the practice of taking action to preserve or improve one's own health, wellbeing, and happiness. It encompasses a wide range of activities and habits that contribute to physical, emotional, and mental health. Orem emphasizes the significance of self-care as "fundamental to the self-care deficit theory, wherein individuals assume responsibility for their health and wellbeing."[3] Additionally, studies in psychology suggest that self-care

1. Oxford Academic (Oxford University Press), "Necessity of Self-Care."
2. Wityk, "Burnout and the Ethics," 4–11.
3. Orem, *Nursing*, 117.

is critical for maintaining mental health, as it helps individuals cope with stressors and emotional challenges.[4] Figley also underscores the role of self-care in professional settings, particularly in high-stress occupations like healthcare and education, where maintaining personal wellbeing is crucial for providing effective care and support to others.[5] Overall, the scholarly consensus is that self-care is a many-sided practice that is vital for sustaining physical, emotional, and mental health.

While self-care is about actively doing things that promote wellbeing, mental hygiene is more about maintaining a "clean mental environment." It's a proactive approach to managing your thoughts, emotions, and reactions. Think of it as brushing your mind the way you brush your teeth: regularly, preventively, and with care. According to Smith and Choudhury, mental hygiene involves practices like cognitive restructuring, mindfulness, and emotional regulation.[6] These help to clear out mental disorders, such as negative thought loops or unhelpful beliefs that can quietly erode your mood and focus. For example, taking a few minutes each morning to center yourself through breathing exercises or gratitude reflection and prayer can help set a positive tone for the day. One of the most powerful tools of mental hygiene is mindfulness—the practice of being present and aware without judgment. Mindfulness not only helps reduce anxiety and stress but also increases emotional regulation and attention.

Integrating Self-Care and Mental Hygiene

While self-care and mental hygiene are distinct, they work best when practiced together. Self-care replenishes your energy and restores your emotional reserves, while mental hygiene keeps your mind clear, focused, and flexible. Together, they form a foundation for resilience and mental wellbeing. Start by integrating small, manageable routines into your day. You don't need an elaborate wellness regimen; just five minutes of deep breathing, a short walk, or turning off notifications after 9 p.m. can make a meaningful difference. What matters is consistency and compassion for yourself.

Self-care is also deeply personal, meaning that what works for one person may not work for another. For some, a daily walk may be calming; for others, journaling or connecting with loved ones is more restorative.

4. Baker, "Self-Care and Mental Health," 145–52.
5. Figley, *Compassion Fatigue*, 10–12.
6. Smith and Choudhury, *Mental Hygiene*, 45–47.

The key is intentionality, choosing activities that replenish your energy and align with your needs, not just distract you from discomfort. Some self-care activities include getting enough sleep, eating well, and exercising, as well as more personalized strategies such as setting boundaries, engaging in hobbies, or practicing mindfulness. Self-care is not a luxury; it's a necessity. According to Pychyl, regular self-care habits act as a "psychological buffer" against stress, helping individuals remain resilient in the face of life's challenges.[7]

THE SIGNIFICANCE OF SELF-CARE FOR COMPANIONS

Accompanying the dying can be emotionally and physically draining. Family, friends, and other caregivers must also care for themselves to remain present and effective. This includes recognizing their own emotions, such as grief and fatigue, and seeking support when needed. Practicing mindfulness, prayer, or other grounding activities can help caregivers process their feelings and maintain balance. Connecting with a support network, whether through friends, family, or professional counselors, provides an outlet for sharing experiences and finding comfort. Self-care is not an indulgence but a necessity, allowing companions to offer their best to the dying person.

Caring for someone at the end of life is emotionally and physically demanding, often requiring long hours, intense emotional engagement, and the capacity to handle grief and loss. Without proper self-care, companions may experience burnout, compassion fatigue, or emotional depletion, which can hinder their ability to remain present and supportive. Taking time to nurture their physical, emotional, and spiritual wellbeing allows caregivers to replenish their energy and maintain the resilience needed to care for others. This can include practices such as regular rest, maintaining healthy boundaries, engaging in spiritual practices, and seeking support from others.

Emotional and psychological self-care is particularly important for companions who are deeply involved in the dying process. The emotions that arise when witnessing suffering or impending death can be overwhelming, especially when there are complex relationships or unresolved emotions with the dying person. Caregivers and companions must learn to process their grief and feelings of helplessness, recognizing that their emotional responses are valid but must be managed to avoid emotional

7. Pychyl, *Psychology of Self-Care*, 88.

exhaustion. Talking with a counselor, joining a support group, or having open conversations with trusted individuals can offer emotional relief and help companions work through their own feelings. Thus, Kübler-Ross notes that caregivers should not feel guilty for taking breaks or seeking professional counseling to manage their grief.[8]

Spiritual self-care is equally vital, especially for those providing pastoral care. Accompanying the dying can challenge one's own faith and bring up questions about mortality, suffering, and the afterlife. Regular practices like prayer, meditation, or reading sacred texts help individuals stay grounded in their faith, enabling them to offer spiritual support to others with authenticity and conviction. By seeking spiritual renewal, care providers are better equipped to hold space for the dying person's spiritual needs, as well as maintain their sense of hope and connection with God. Research suggests that when care providers practice self-care, they are better able to offer compassionate and present-centered support to the dying.[9] Ultimately, by prioritizing their wellbeing, they can foster resilience and continue to provide meaningful, loving care without compromising their own mental and emotional health. Some forms of self-care include:

Practical Self-Care

Practical self-care entails engaging in activities and adopting habits that make everyday life more manageable and reduce stress by maintaining order and efficiency. This includes organizing one's living and working spaces to create a clutter-free and functional environment, which can enhance focus and reduce anxiety. Effective time management practices, such as planning and prioritizing tasks, help balance responsibilities and leisure, ensuring that important activities are completed without overwhelming oneself. Financial self-care is another crucial aspect, involving budgeting, saving, and managing expenses to achieve financial stability and reduce money-related stress. Additionally, practical self-care can include maintaining a work-life balance, setting realistic goals, and seeking professional help when necessary to manage tasks and responsibilities efficiently.

- **Organization:** Keeping your living and working spaces organized to reduce stress.

8. Kübler-Ross, *On Death and Dying*, 175.
9. Stroebe et al., *Handbook of Bereavement*, 209.

- **Time Management:** Planning and managing your time to balance responsibilities and leisure.
- **Financial Health:** Managing your finances to reduce stress and build security.

Physical Self-Care

Physical self-care involves taking proactive steps to maintain and improve one's physical health and wellbeing. This includes engaging in regular exercise to stay fit and release endorphins (i.e., relieve pain, enhance mood, feel-good hormones, etc.), eating a balanced and nutritious diet to fuel the body, ensuring adequate sleep for rest and recovery, staying hydrated by drinking enough water, and attending regular healthcare checkups to monitor and address any health concerns. By prioritizing these activities, individuals can enhance their overall physical health, boost their energy levels, and reduce the risk of illness.

- **Exercise:** Regular physical activity, such as walking, running, yoga, or strength training, helps maintain physical health and releases endorphins.
- **Nutrition:** Eating a balanced diet rich in fruits, vegetables, whole grains, and lean proteins.
- **Sleep:** Getting enough quality sleep to support overall health and function.
- **Hydration:** Drinking enough water throughout the day.
- **Healthcare:** Regular checkups, and managing health conditions before they become chronic.

Emotional Self-Care

Caring for oneself emotionally involves engaging in activities and practices that promote emotional wellbeing and resilience. This includes managing stress through mindfulness, meditation, or deep breathing exercises; expressing emotions in healthy ways, such as journaling or speaking with a trusted friend or therapist; and setting boundaries to protect oneself from emotional overload. It also involves recognizing and validating one's own feelings, practicing self-compassion, and seeking support when needed.

- **Stress Management:** Practices such as mindfulness, meditation, or deep breathing exercises.
- **Emotional Expression:** Allowing yourself to express emotions through journaling, talking to a friend, or seeing a therapist.
- **Boundaries:** Setting and maintaining healthy boundaries in personal and professional relationships.

Mental Self-Care

Caring for oneself mentally involves engaging in activities that stimulate and maintain cognitive health and mental clarity. This includes lifelong learning through reading, solving puzzles, or acquiring new skills, as well as fostering creativity through artistic endeavors like drawing or writing. Practicing mindfulness and meditation helps maintain mental focus and reduce anxiety. Additionally, taking breaks and allowing time for rest and relaxation are crucial for preventing mental fatigue.

- **Learning:** Engaging in activities that stimulate the mind, such as reading, puzzles, or learning new skills.
- **Creativity:** Participating in creative activities like drawing, painting, writing, playing music, or watching videos.
- **Mindfulness:** Practicing mindfulness or meditation to stay present and reduce anxiety.

Social Self-Care

Socializing as a means of self-care involves engaging in meaningful interactions and building relationships with others to enhance emotional and mental wellbeing. Regular social activities, whether with friends, family, or community groups, provide support, reduce feelings of loneliness, and foster a sense of belonging. Positive social interactions can boost mood, increase feelings of happiness, and provide opportunities for sharing experiences and gaining different perspectives. Engaging in social self-care also helps develop communication skills, build a support network, and create a balance between work and personal life.

- **Relationships:** Maintaining healthy, supportive relationships with friends, family, and loved ones.
- **Social Activities:** Participating in social activities and community events.
- **Communication:** Practicing effective communication and reaching out for support when needed.

Spiritual Self-Care

Caring for oneself spiritually involves engaging in practices and activities that nurture one's sense of meaning, purpose, and connection to something greater than oneself. This can include meditation, prayer, or attending religious or spiritual services, which help cultivate inner peace and reflection. Spending time in nature, practicing gratitude, and engaging in activities that align with personal values and beliefs also contribute to spiritual well-being. Additionally, exploring philosophical or spiritual texts, participating in community service, and connecting with like-minded individuals can deepen one's spiritual understanding and fulfillment.

- **Reflection:** Engaging in practices like prayer, meditation, or journaling to reflect on your values and purpose, and retreat.
- **Nature:** Spending time in nature to connect with the environment and find peace.
- **Gratitude:** Practicing gratitude by acknowledging and appreciating the positives in your life.

BENEFITS OF PRACTICING HOLISTIC SELF-CARE

Practicing holistic self-care offers a range of benefits that contribute to overall wellbeing by addressing physical, emotional, mental, social, and spiritual aspects of life. Here are some key benefits:

1. **Enhanced Physical Health:** Holistic self-care promotes physical health through balanced nutrition, regular exercise, adequate sleep,

and preventive healthcare, which can lead to improved immune function, increased energy levels, and a lower risk of chronic diseases. Wicks opines that looking at what element nourishes one is better than feeding oneself with whatever crosses one's path.[10] One feels better both spiritually and physically when one eats less. Occasionally, going to bed slightly hungry does many beneficial things for one's body and soul. In most cases, gluttonousness and the habit of eating junk food come into play when one overworks him/herself and becomes too tired to prepare a healthy meal.

2. **Improved Emotional Resilience:** Engaging in emotional self-care practices like mindfulness, journaling, and therapy helps manage stress, process emotions, and build resilience, leading to better emotional stability and a more positive outlook on life.
3. **Better Mental Clarity and Cognitive Function:** Mental self-care activities, including skill acquisition, creative engagement, and mindfulness practice, strengthen cognitive function, improve problem-solving capabilities, and elevate general mental clarity.
4. **Stronger Social Connections:** Prioritizing social self-care through significant encounters and the cultivation of supportive connections enhances individuals' sense of belonging, diminishes feelings of loneliness, and bolsters emotional support.
5. **Deeper Spiritual Fulfillment:** Spiritual self-care practices, such as meditation, reflection, and engaging with one's beliefs, encourage a sense of accomplishment, inner peace, and connection to something greater, which can enhance overall life satisfaction.
6. **Increased Self-Awareness:** Holistic self-care encourages self-reflection and self-compassion, helping individuals develop a greater appreciation for their needs, desires, and goals, which promotes personal growth and self-improvement.
7. **Balanced Life:** A holistic approach to self-care addresses multiple dimensions of wellbeing; this includes helping to create a balanced and fulfilling life where physical health, emotional stability, mental engagement, social connections, and spiritual fulfillment are all nurtured.

10. Wicks, "The Necessity of Self-Care" (video), xx.

8. **Stress Reduction and Better Coping Skills:** Holistic self-care provides tools and techniques for managing stress, such as relaxation exercises, time management, and emotional expression, which can improve coping mechanisms and reduce overall stress levels.
9. **Prevention of Burnout:** Regularly engaging in self-care practices helps prevent burnout by maintaining a sustainable balance between work, personal life, and self-care activities, leading to increased satisfaction and motivation. Scalise cited Dr. Hart's comment that "burnout may never kill you, but your long life may not seem like living. But stress will kill you prematurely, and you won't have enough time to finish what you started."[11] With this being said, there is a need for self-care; otherwise, one could experience burnout. Accordingly, Moitinho says that stress is a reality and does affect our bodies.[12] He made very clear points on the need for one to manage stress properly to avoid burnout.
10. **Overall Wellbeing:** By addressing the complete range of self-care requirements, individuals attain a more holistic sense of wellbeing, whereby physical health, emotional stability, mental acuity, social support, and spiritual connection are all integrated.

Final Thoughts

Prioritizing mental health is not an act of selfishness. Engaging in self-care and mental hygiene enhances your wellbeing and enables you to assist others effectively. In an era marked by escalating burnout and worry, these activities have become increasingly vital. For instance, when feeling overwhelmed, pause, breathe, and safeguard your tranquility. Engaging in a tranquil walk, perusing an engrossing narrative or inspirational literature, viewing an enjoyable film, exercising, and consuming nutritious food are supplementary methods of self-care. Scalise emphasizes the need to pay attention to diet, exercise, and having some silent moments.[13] He asserts that there is an abundance of joy and peace in God's presence. Therefore, when one is dealing with lots of worries and unable to find joy, one can get into God's presence for some quiet, spiritual, and physical renewal.[14] As a

11. Scalise, *When Helping You Is Hurting Me.*
12. Moitinho, "Understanding Stress and Burnout."
13. Scalise, *When Helping You Is Hurting Me.*
14. Scalise, *When Helping You Is Hurting Me.*

matter of fact, in prayer one can be inspired on how to deal with certain life situations than worry sick about them. Thus, 1 Pet 5:7 (NIV) says: "Cast all your anxiety on him because he cares for you."

Tips for Effective Self-Care

1. **Identify Your Needs:** Understand what aspects of self-care are most important to you.
2. **Create a Routine:** Integrate self-care practices into your daily or weekly routine.
3. **Be Consistent:** Consistency is key to reaping the benefits of self-care.
4. **Be Kind to Yourself:** Practice self-compassion and avoid being too critical of yourself.
5. **Seek Professional Help:** Don't hesitate to seek help from healthcare providers, therapists, or counselors if needed.
6. **Be Compassionate**
7. **Learn to Forgive, Letting Go and Letting God**
8. **Build a Personal Relationship with a Higher Power**

PART III

Hope Beyond the Horizon

9

Where Death Meets Resurrection

(The Hope That Holds Us)

STORY: THE LIGHT OF HOPE

In a small town, there lived an old clockmaker named Jose. His shop, filled with the gentle ticking of hundreds of timepieces, sat on the corner of Main Street like a quiet hymn to time itself. People said Jose could fix anything, grandfather clocks, wristwatches, even hearts, if you stayed long enough to talk to him.

One bright morning, a young woman named Flora walked into Jose's shop. She was a scientist, brilliant, skeptical, and recently diagnosed with an aggressive illness. Her days, like the clocks around her, now felt numbered.

"I don't believe in anything after all," she told Jose bluntly. "I just wanted to see your clocks before I go."

Jose, who had buried his wife the year before, only nodded and handed her a delicate timepiece. "Then let's talk about what we do while the clock still ticks," Jose said.

Over the weeks, Flora began to visit Jose regularly. They talked about science, the stars, entropy, and poetry. She spoke of the futility she felt, how the vast universe seemed indifferent to her little life. Jose listened with a patience refined over years of tuning the heartbeat of gears.

One day, Flora asked, "Do you really believe there's something after death?"

"I do," Jose replied. "But hope isn't just about what comes after. It's about how we live while we're here."

He told her about his faith, not as an escape from death, but as a lens that made the ordinary sacred. "Hope," he said, "is not the denial of death. It's the stubborn belief that love and meaning outlast even it."

Flora frowned. "But I can't believe in God."

Jose smiled gently. "Hope isn't owned by faith alone. It's in every act of kindness, every moment you choose to love despite the ending."

One peaceful evening, Jose gave Flora a gift: a small pocket watch, its back engraved with the words "Still, the light comes."

"The light of hope," he said. "In the face of death, light still comes. Maybe from God. Maybe from us. Maybe that's enough."

Reflection: *In the face of human mortality, one of the most profound and universal questions that has occupied the human spirit is how to cultivate hope in the midst of inevitable death. The reality of death, its inescapable nature, and the grief that accompanies it can lead to despair, but within the framework of Christian theology, hope remains a central tenet that offers comfort and meaning. A theology of hope amid mortality does not ignore the reality of death but instead provides a lens through which the experience of death can be understood in light of divine promises, resurrection, and eternal life.*

LIVING WITH HOPE, EVEN AS WE DIE

At its core, hope is a confident expectation of future fulfillment, grounded in the promises of God. Within the framework of mortality, hope establishes a basis for embracing the understanding that death, although a universal and inevitable aspect of existence, holds no ultimate authority. The apostle Paul articulates this vision of hope in 1 Cor 15:54–55, where he proclaims, "Death has been swallowed up in victory. Where, O death, is your victory? Where, O death, is your sting?" Through the lens of Christian theology, hope in the face of death is not merely a wish for life to be different but a confident trust in God's eternal promises. Hope is both a present reality and a future expectation, rooted in the resurrection of Jesus Christ.

Christian hope acknowledges the sorrow and pain of mortality, yet it holds to the belief that the end of life on earth is not the end of the story. Jesus' death and resurrection are considered the ultimate victory over sin and death, making a way for believers to anticipate a future resurrection. This hope is spiritual and theological, but not abstract; it comforts and encourages those dealing with grief, suffering, and the reality of their own or their loved ones' mortality.

The Resurrection: Anchor of Hope

The resurrection of Jesus Christ lies at the heart of the Christian hope amidst mortality. Christianity does not present a view of death as final or as the end of all things. Instead, it declares that death has been conquered through the resurrection of Christ, offering hope to all who believe in him. The resurrection assures believers that physical death is not the ultimate end but a passage into eternal life. Jesus' victory over death offers a radical transformation of how Christians understand mortality. In the Gospels, Jesus' death is not viewed as a tragic end but as the means by which the world is redeemed. Luke 24:26: "Was it not necessary that the Christ should suffer these things and enter into his glory?" His resurrection is the firstfruits of a new creation, and it assures Christians that they too will share in this victory over death. This promise is not just about the afterlife but about the transformation of the present reality. Christians understand that, in the face of mortality, there is a deeper hope that transcends human limitations and speaks to the final restoration of all things.

For many Christians, the hope of resurrection shapes their lives in profound ways. It gives meaning to suffering, offering the assurance that, like Christ, those who suffer in this life will experience renewal and restoration in the life to come. The apostle Paul writes in Rom 8:18 that "the sufferings of this present time are not worth comparing with the glory that is to be revealed to us." In the context of mortality, the theology of resurrection urges individuals to live in accordance with the hope that suffering and death are transient, and that the ensuing eternal glory will significantly surpass the temporal pain of this world.

Hope and Grief: A Tension of Faith and Emotion

One of the most difficult aspects of mortality is the experience of grief. The loss of a loved one brings sorrow, pain, and a sense of finality that can feel overwhelming. A theology of hope does not deny the reality of grief but offers a way to integrate sorrow with the promise of comfort and eternal life. In John 11, the story of Jesus' encounter with the grieving sisters Mary and Martha over the death of their brother Lazarus exemplifies this balance of hope and grief. Jesus expresses sorrow at Lazarus' death, yet he also declares, "I am the resurrection and the life. The one who believes in me will live, even though they die" (John 11:25). In this passage, hope and grief are held together. Jesus does not dismiss the reality of grief but provides the hope of resurrection and eternal life, offering a model for Christians who mourn in the face of mortality.

Hope amid mortality allows the grieving person to experience their sorrow fully while also being held by the promise that death does not have the final say. The Christian hope is one that provides deep emotional comfort in the midst of loss, offering assurance that those who have died will be raised to life again. This hope does not erase the pain of death; it provides a framework through which believers can find peace and strength, knowing that death is temporary and that they will be reunited with their loved ones in eternity.

Ultimate Hope: Resurrection and Renewal

The hope offered by Christianity extends beyond the individual and embraces the entire created order. The death and resurrection of Jesus Christ are considered the beginning of a new creation, where all things will be made new. Revelation 21:4 speaks of a time when God "will wipe every tear from their eyes. There will be no more death or mourning or crying or pain, for the old order of things has passed away." In a theology of hope, mortality is viewed not as a cyclical or meaningless experience but as part of God's larger redemptive plan for the world. Thus, Moltmann emphasizes that "in the eschatological renewal of the world, the resurrection of Christ becomes the principle of hope for the transformation of all reality. He insists that hope is not escapism but rather "an active power to work toward a better future within history."[1]

This vision of eternal life and the renewal of all things shapes the Christian's approach to mortality. It invites believers to live with the hope that suffering, death, and decay are not the final word. Rather, they are part of the process of redemption that God will ultimately complete when Christ returns. The hope of eternal life is not simply about escaping death but about the complete renewal of the world, where God's justice, peace, and love will reign. In this renewed world, death will be no more, and all things will be restored to their intended purpose. This vision provides hope not only for personal salvation but also for the healing and restoration of the entire world, which is a central part of Christian eschatological hope.

Living with Hope in the Present

A theology of hope amid mortality also affects how individuals live in the present. While Christian hope assures believers of eternal life after death, it also calls them to live with that hope in the here and now. In light of the resurrection, Christians are invited to live as "resurrection people," reflecting God's hope and transformation in their daily lives. This includes embodying love, justice, and mercy in the world, knowing that these actions are part of God's redemptive work on earth. It involves embracing life in the face of death, finding joy in the midst of suffering, and offering comfort to others who grieve.

In the context of mortality, hope encourages individuals to live fully, knowing that death is not the end but a transition into a fuller experience of life with God. Christians are called to care for others, serve the vulnerable, and work toward a more just and peaceful world, motivated by the hope that God's kingdom is coming. The hope of resurrection does not lead to passivity or resignation but to active engagement in life and in the work of God's kingdom.

1. Moltmann, *Theology of Hope*, 218.

THE ROLE OF ESCHATOLOGICAL HOPE

Eschatological hope stands at the heart of Christian theology, shaping how believers understand both the future and their present responsibilities. Far from being abstract speculation about the end times, it affirms that history is moving toward God's promised renewal of all things. As Wright explains, Christian hope is rooted in the resurrection of Jesus Christ, which serves not only as a guarantee of life after death but also as a declaration that God intends to restore and redeem creation itself.[2] This hope resists distracting tendencies by emphasizing that God's kingdom is coming and calling the church to embody that future now through faithful witness and service.[3]

More than just consolation, eschatological hope empowers the church to persevere amid suffering and to work for justice and peace in a fallen world. According to Moltmann, "From first to last . . . Christianity is eschatology; it is hope." He argues that this future-oriented faith is not passive waiting but a dynamic force that shapes ethical action and inspires transformative engagement with the world.[4] Believers are thus not merely waiting for heaven but actively participating in God's redemptive mission. Through eschatological hope, Christians live in the tension between the "already" and the "not yet," trusting that the future God has promised gives meaning, direction, and courage in the present.

Eschatological Hope as Comfort Amid Suffering

One of the primary functions of eschatological hope in pastoral care is to provide comfort in the face of suffering. Life often confronts individuals with pain, illness, grief, and the fear of death, leading many to question the purpose of their experiences and the nature of God's presence. In such moments, the Christian promise of a future free from suffering, where God "will wipe every tear from their eyes" and "there will be no more death or mourning or crying or pain" (Rev 21:4), offers profound reassurance. Therefore, suffering is not to separate one from God (Rom 8:39). Instead, it challenges the boundaries of one's relationships with God and others.[5]

2. Wright, *Surprised by Hope*, 202–4.
3. Wright, *Surprised by Hope*, 25.
4. Moltmann, *Theology of Hope*, 328.
5. Zylla, *Roots of Sorrow*, 126.

Thus, John 16:33 encourages Christians to take heart and be assured God has overcome the world no matter the troubles.

Pastoral caregivers, guided by eschatological hope, help individuals reframe their suffering in the context of God's eternal plan. While it does not diminish the reality or intensity of pain, it encourages the belief that suffering is temporary and that God is working toward a future where all things will be made right. This assurance can help individuals endure their present struggles with faith and perseverance, knowing that their pain is not meaningless but part of a larger redemptive story.

Eschatological Hope and Grief

In times of loss, eschatological hope offers a powerful response to the finality of death. Grieving individuals often wrestle with the separation from their loved ones and the seeming permanence of death. Eschatological hope provides a vision of reunion and restoration, as promised in the resurrection of the dead and the life everlasting. The Christian belief in resurrection, grounded in Jesus Christ's own victory over death, assures the bereaved that death is not the end but a transition into eternal life with God. Caregivers who emphasize eschatological hope can bring comfort to the grieving by helping them focus on the promise of eternal reunion with their loved ones and the joy of being in God's presence.

Hope and Meaning in Life's Deepest Questions

To resolve the existential and ethical dilemmas that come up in hospital settings, eschatological hope plays a critical role. People who are dealing with a terminal disease, a diagnosis that changes their life, or a significant loss may wonder about the meaning of life and whether their situation is fair. Eschatological hope serves as a reminder to believers that this life is not the end and that the difficulties that individuals face now are a necessary part of a path to a more glorious existence. For example, in end-of-life care, eschatological hope helps individuals approach death not with fear but with trust in God's promises. It reframes the end of earthly life as a step into eternal communion with God, alleviating the anxiety and despair that often accompany dying.

Eschatological Hope and Resilience

Another critical role of eschatological hope in pastoral care is fostering resilience. Life's challenges, from chronic illness to societal unrest, can weaken individuals' and families' ability to persevere. Eschatological hope provides the strength to endure by anchoring faith in God's unchanging promises. The belief that God's purposes will ultimately prevail instills a sense of purpose and determination to keep moving forward, even when circumstances seem bleak. Caregiving, rooted in eschatological hope, equips individuals to trust in God's sovereignty and faithfulness. By focusing on the certainty of God's redemptive plan, caregivers can help individuals and families develop the spiritual resources needed to navigate their challenges with courage and grace.

The Transformative Power of Eschatological Hope

Ultimately, eschatological hope is transformative. It invites individuals, families, and friends to live in the present with an eternal perspective, shaping how they approach suffering, relationships, and their responsibilities in the world. Far from encouraging passivity, this hope inspires believers to work toward God's kingdom on earth, addressing suffering and injustice with the confidence that their efforts are part of God's redemptive work. This hope is a powerful tool for inspiring both faith and action. It calls individuals to trust in God's promises while actively participating in the healing and reconciliation of the world. By integrating this hope into the ministry of care, caregivers help those they serve to live with a sense of purpose and anticipation, rooted in the belief that God is making all things new.

FAITH AND TRUST IN GOD'S PRESENCE THROUGH DEATH

Story 2: The Final Walk

There lived an old man named Abel. He was known not for his wealth or strength, but for his deep and unwavering faith in God. His life had seen many losses: his wife, his son in war, and most recently, his sight. Yet Abel was never bitter. People often asked him how he managed to remain so calm, so trusting, even in grief.

One evening, word spread that Abel was dying. The villagers, out of love and respect, came to visit. Among them was a boy named Bobo, whose father had recently passed away. Bobo was angry at God, confused and heartbroken. He approached Abel, tears brimming in his eyes.

"Why does God take people? Why did He take my father?" Bobo asked. "How can you still believe in Him after losing so much?"

Abel reached for Bobo's hand and smiled gently. "Let me tell you a story, child."

He paused, then began in his slow, gravelly voice:

"When I was young, my father would take me on walks through these forests. On one walk, night fell faster than we expected. I was scared; I couldn't see anything, and the woods felt full of danger. But my father took my hand and said, 'Trust me. I know the way.'

"I couldn't see him. I couldn't even see the path. But I trusted him, because he was my father. And step by step, though it was dark and cold, he brought me home.

"Death is like that walk, Bobo. It may feel dark and lonely. But I know just as surely as I knew my father's hand that God is with us. Even when we can't see Him, we are not alone."

Tears welled in Bobo's eyes, but this time they were not just of grief; they were mixed with hope.

That night, Abel passed peacefully in his sleep.

At his funeral, Bobo stood quietly by the casket, looking up at the sky.

He whispered, "I'll trust You, even when I can't see."

And from that moment, the seed of faith grew in his young heart, faith that God walks with us, even through death, leading us home.

The journey through death, whether one's own or that of a loved one, can be a time of profound spiritual challenge and transformation. Amid the sorrow, fear, and uncertainty that often accompany death, faith in God's abiding presence provides a wellspring of hope and peace. Pastors, caregivers and Christian teaching play a vital role in inspiring people's faith and trust in God during these moments, reassuring them that God's love and promises remain steadfast even in the face of mortality.

Scripture consistently affirms that God's presence is constant, even in life's darkest moments. The psalmist declares, "Even though I walk through the valley of the shadow of death, I will fear no evil, for you are with me" (Ps 23:4). This assurance of divine companionship speaks directly to the human experience of death, reminding believers that they are never abandoned. Emphasizing God's unwavering presence helps to counter the isolation and fear that can arise during terminal illness, the dying process, or grief.

For those facing their death, trusting in God's presence provides the courage to approach the end of life with peace rather than fear. This trust can be nurtured by prayer, reflection on Scripture, and the sacraments, particularly the Eucharist and Anointing of the Sick, which serve as tangible signs of God's nearness. For grieving families, remembering that God is faithful can help navigate the emotional upheaval of loss and provide comfort in the knowledge that their loved one is in God's care, and that they, too, are upheld by His love.

Jesus' Example: Death as a Passage, Not an End

The life, death, and resurrection of Jesus Christ form the foundation for Christian faith and trust in God's presence through death. In Jesus, people see that God does not remain distant from human suffering and mortality but enters into it fully, transforming it from within. Jesus' words on the cross, "Father, into your hands I commit my spirit" (Luke 23:46), model a profound trust in God, even in the face of death. Caregivers can draw on Jesus' example to inspire faith in God's redemptive purposes. Death, though deeply painful, is not the end but a passage into eternal life with God. By reflecting on Jesus' victory over death, believers are encouraged to see their mortality in the light of resurrection and eternal life. This perspective reframes death not as a loss of God's presence but as the ultimate realization of His promise to bring His children into everlasting communion with Him.

The Role of Prayer and Worship

Prayer and worship are powerful practices for fostering faith and trust in God's presence through death. Prayers of lament allow individuals to express their sorrow and fear honestly, while prayers of trust affirm God's sovereignty and love. Worship, particularly in the context of a faith community, reinforces the assurance of God's presence through hymns, Scripture readings, and the shared proclamation of hope in Christ. For those nearing the end of life, pastoral caregivers can guide them in prayers that express surrender to God and reliance on His care. Practices such as reciting the

Lord's Prayer, meditating on Ps 23, or participating in the Sacrament of Reconciliation can help individuals attain peace.

Faith in the Face of Mystery

One of the greatest challenges in inspiring faith and trust in God during death is addressing the mystery surrounding mortality. Questions about the "why" of suffering, the nature of life after death, and God's role in the dying process can unsettle even the most steadfast believers. Christian teaching assures believers that God's ways are higher than human understanding (Isa 55:8–9). This acknowledgment of mystery invites individuals to trust not in their ability to comprehend but in God's character as loving, faithful, and sovereign. Caregivers can help individuals and families lean into this trust by encouraging them to rest in the assurance that God's presence is real, even when the path forward is unclear.

Signs of God's Presence in the Dying Process

The dying process itself can be a sacred time where God's presence is deeply felt. Many individuals and families report experiences of spiritual clarity, moments of peace, or a sense of divine closeness in the final stages of life. Pastors can help people recognize these signs of God's presence, whether through the comfort of loved ones, the beauty of creation, or a profound sense of inner peace. Sacred rituals, such as anointing with oil, reading Scripture, or sharing Communion, also serve as powerful reminders of God's nearness. These practices affirm that God is actively present in the transition from earthly life to eternal life, guiding the dying person gently into His care.

Hope in the Promise of Resurrection

The fundamental basis of faith and confidence in God's presence during death is the assurance of resurrection. Christian hope is founded on the conviction that death is not definitive; through the resurrection of Jesus, eternal life is guaranteed for all believers. This assurance establishes the basis for bravery and tranquility as individuals confront mortality. The care team can assist individuals and families in grounding themselves in hope by emphasizing Scripture passages that affirm God's promises, such as John 11:25 ("I am the resurrection and the life"), 1 Thess 4:14 ("For we believe that Jesus died and rose again"), and Rev 21:4, reminding Christians that their faith in God is well founded and that His presence during death leads to eternal life.

Conclusively, inspiring faith and trust in God's presence through death is a sacred responsibility that draws deeply on the truths of Christian theology and the lived experience of God's faithfulness. By emphasizing God's constant presence, the victory of Jesus over death, the power of prayer and worship, and the hope of resurrection, individuals can be comforted and strengthened when facing the profound realities of mortality. Faith in God, even in the shadow of death, transforms fear into peace, sorrow into hope, and endings into new beginnings in His eternal love.

10

Death, Not an End

(A Final Word of Courage and Grace)

STORY: THE WINDING PATH

Once upon a time, in a distant land lived a young woman named Amara. She dreamed of reaching the Horizon Flame, a mysterious golden glow that shimmered on the edge of the world. The elders said it was not a place, but a promise. Those who reached it found peace, purpose, and something beyond what eyes could see.

On her twentieth birthday, Amara set out on the path that led toward the glow. It started wide and easy, filled with sunlight and birdsong. Her heart was light. She thought, "This will be simple."

But the path twisted.

Soon, it led into dense forests where thorns scraped her skin and shadows whispered doubts. She stumbled over roots and cried in the dark. There were times she considered turning back. But each time, she remembered the glow. And each time she rose, she felt a little stronger.

As the years passed, the path wound through many places: deserts where her strength was tested, mountains that demanded courage, and valleys where she met fellow travelers, some who joined her, some who departed. She bore losses, learned patience, offered help, and received it.

One day, after what felt like a lifetime of walking, Amara found herself at the edge of a cliff. Below stretched clouds painted with gold and crimson. She had aged, her hair streaked with silver, her hands worn. Yet the glow that once seemed far away now bathed her in light.

She wept, not because the journey was over, but because it had made her who she was.

From behind her, a young traveler appeared, lost and tired. Amara turned, smiled, and offered her hand.

"Is that the Horizon Flame?" the traveler asked, pointing to the light.

"Yes," Amara said, eyes shining. "And no. It's ahead, always. But it's also within you, growing every time you choose to keep walking."

The path went on. The glow remained. And so did hope, the quiet promise that every twist and trial shapes the soul, guiding it toward something greater.

Standing on the Promises of God

1. Standing on the promises of Christ my King,
Through eternal ages let His praises ring;
Glory in the highest, I will shout and sing,
Standing on the promises of God.

Refrain:
Standing, standing,
Standing on the promises of God my Savior;
Standing, standing,
I'm standing on the promises of God.

2. Standing on the promises that cannot fail,
When the howling storms of doubt and fear assail,
By the living Word of God I shall prevail,
Standing on the promises of God.

Refrain

3. Standing on the promises of Christ the Lord,
Bound to Him eternally by love's strong cord,
Overcoming daily with the Spirit's sword,
Standing on the promises of God.

Refrain

4. Standing on the promises I cannot fall,
Listening every moment to the Spirit's call,
Resting in my Savior as my all in all,
Standing on the promises of God.

Refrain

"Standing on the Promises of God" is a hymn of steadfast faith and enduring hope. Written by Russell Kelso Carter in 1886, it reminds Christians that God's promises are unchanging and reliable, even when life is full of trials, doubts, or uncertainty. The imagery of "standing" conveys strength, persistence, and trust, encouraging Christians to anchor their lives in God's Word. Each stanza emphasizes reliance on God's power, the sustaining nature of His Spirit, and the assurance that He will never fail. This hymn inspires resilience, reminding us that spiritual victories and peace are possible when we remain grounded in God's promises, despite the storms of life.

Amazing Grace:

Verse 1:
Amazing grace! (how sweet the sound)
That saved a wretch like me!
I once was lost, but now am found,
Was blind, but now I see.

Verse 2:
'Twas grace that taught my heart to fear,
And grace my fears relieved;
How precious did that grace appear
The hour I first believed!

Verse 3:
Through many dangers, toils and snares,
I have already come;
'Tis grace hath brought me safe thus far,
And grace will lead me home.

Verse 4:
The Lord has promised good to me,
His word my hope secures;
He will my shield and portion be,
As long as life endures.

Verse 5:
Yea, when this flesh and heart shall fail,
And mortal life shall cease,
I shall possess, within the veil,
A life of joy and peace.

Verse 6:
When we've been there ten thousand years
Bright shining as the sun,
We've no less days to sing God's praise
Than when we first begun.

"Amazing Grace," too, is one of the most well-known and beloved hymns in the English-speaking world, written by John Newton (1725–1807). He was a former slave ship captain who converted to Christianity and later became an Anglican clergyman and abolitionist. He wrote "Amazing Grace" in 1772 as a reflection on his personal transformation and redemption. It was first published by anonymously in 1829. The melody most commonly associated with the hymn today, called "New Britain," was added later and first appeared in William Walker's 1835 songbook Southern Harmony.

As this journey concludes, it affirms a central truth: death is not the end. In Christ, death has been overcome, and life eternal awaits. This truth empowers everyone to walk this path with courage and faith, knowing that

God is always with them, bringing beauty from ashes and life from death. Together, as the body of Christ, we proclaim with confidence, "O death, where is your victory? O grave, where is your sting?" (1 Cor 15:55). The journey may be marked by sorrow, but it is ultimately a journey of hope, a hope that rests in the unchanging love and eternal promises of God.

The journey of exploring death and dying through the lens of pastoral care is an invitation to confront some of the most profound aspects of human existence. It is a path marked by sorrow, mystery, and questions, but also one filled with opportunities for deep comfort and abiding hope. At its heart, this journey seeks to embrace the reality of mortality while pointing to the greater truths of God's love, presence, and promises. It is a ministry of accompaniment, where the caregiver becomes a reflection of God's compassion, walking alongside individuals and families in their moments of deepest vulnerability.

To accompany someone in their final days is a sacred privilege. It is a call to offer more than practical help or emotional support; it is an opportunity to become a vessel of God's peace, embodying the assurance of His presence even in the face of death. Caregivers in these moments must recognize the inherent dignity of every individual, affirming that they are beloved children of God. Through prayer, ritual, and attentive presence, caregivers provide the dying with the reassurance that they are neither alone nor forgotten. This care extends to their loved ones, creating a space where grief, fear, and uncertainty can be expressed and held within the greater promise of God's faithfulness.

Comfort is a central pillar of caregiving in the context of death and dying. It is not a promise to erase pain but an invitation to face it within a framework of love and support. By listening deeply, offering empathy, and providing spiritual guidance, pastoral caregivers help those in their care find moments of peace amid the turmoil. A caregiver provides clarity and strength when families need it most, whether they are navigating complex decisions or guiding them through anticipatory grief. It reminds all involved that, even in the shadow of death, God is present and active, bringing His light into the darkest moments.

At the same time, the journey of pastoral care is one of proclaiming hope. This hope is not a denial of death's reality but a firm belief in the promises of resurrection and eternal life. Grounded in the victory of Jesus Christ, hope allows individuals to approach death with faith rather than fear, seeing it as a transition rather than an end. The care team becomes bearers of this hope, weaving it into prayers, conversations, and rituals that connect the present moment to the ultimate reality of God's redemptive plan. For grieving families, this hope serves as an anchor, reminding them that death does not sever the bonds of love but transforms them into something eternal.

Grief, though painful, is also a transformative process. For those who remain, the loss of a loved one is a journey through sorrow toward healing and renewal. Caregiving does not end with death but continues into the days, weeks, and months that follow, as individuals and families navigate life without their loved ones. Through ongoing support, counseling, and the rituals of remembrance, caregivers help the bereaved recognize meaning in their loss, encouraging them to see their grief as part of a larger story of love, faith, and hope. The church, as a community of faith, plays an essential role here, offering a space where grief can be shared and comfort found in the presence of others.

Death and dying are never experienced in isolation. They impact families, friends, and communities, creating ripples that extend far beyond the individual. The faith community is called to be a source of strength and solace, reminding all who mourn that they are part of a larger body that carries their burdens and celebrates their joys. Through shared worship, acts of service, and communal prayer, the church becomes a living testament to the truth of God's promises, proclaiming that, in Christ, death has been conquered and life eternal awaits.

Ultimately, the intersection of mortality signifies a journey beyond itself. It is not only a confrontation with death but also an invitation to live with eternity in view. For the dying, it is a time to entrust their lives fully into God's hands, resting in the assurance of His love. For the living, it is an opportunity to honor those who have gone before while embracing their own lives with renewed faith and purpose. This dual perspective, rooted in the hope of resurrection, transforms the way we approach both life and death.

As this exploration concludes, we are reminded that death, though deeply challenging, is not the final word. Through Christ's victory over the grave, we are assured that life continues in the presence of God, where every tear is wiped away, and all things are made new. This truth empowers us to face death with courage and faith, knowing that God walks with us every step of the way. The pastoral journey of comfort and hope is ultimately one of trust, trust in the God who is always present, always loving, and always faithful. In this trust, we find peace for the present, strength for the journey, and hope for the life to come.

Appendix 1

Prayers and Scriptural Readings for End-of-Life Care

PRAYERS

1. ***A Prayer for Peace for the Dying***
   Heavenly Father,
   You are the giver of life and the sustainer of all creation. In this sacred moment, we entrust [Name] into Your loving care. Bring peace to his/her heart, calm to his/her spirit, and comfort to his/her body. Surround him/her with Your presence, reminding him/her that he/she is not alone. May Your grace carry him/her gently from this life into the fullness of eternal life with You. In God's name we pray. Amen.

2. ***A Prayer for Strength for the Family***
   Gracious God,
   In this time of sorrow and uncertainty, we lift up [Name/family] to You. Give (us) them strength and courage as (we) they walk this difficult journey. Comfort (us) them with the assurance of Your love and the hope of resurrection. May (we) they feel Your arms around (us) them, supporting (us) them in their grief, and give (us) them peace that surpasses understanding. In Your name, we pray. Amen.

3. ***A Prayer for Reconciliation***
   Merciful God,
   In this moment of transition, we ask for Your healing touch upon this family. If there are words left unspoken or wounds left unhealed, bring Your forgiveness and grace. May [Name] and his/her loved ones

experience a sense of closure, reconciliation, and peace. Let Your Spirit guide (us) them toward love and understanding, so (we) they may be free to rest in You. We pray in God's name. Amen.

4. ***A Prayer to Accompany a Departed Loved One Home***

O God of Life and Light,

We come before You today with hearts that are heavy, yet full of gratitude for the life of Your beloved child, [Name], who now returns to You. Thank You, dear God, for the time we shared, for the love we gave and received, for every moment of laughter and comfort, for the touch of his/her hand, the sound of his/her voice, and the kindness in his/her eyes. These memories are treasures that will remain in our hearts, even as [Name] journeys beyond the veil of this earthly life.

You are the Alpha and the Omega, the Beginning and the End. You breathed life into our beloved one, and now You receive him/her into Your eternal arms. Though we grieve, we take comfort in Your promises, that death is not the end, but the threshold of a new and everlasting life in Your presence.

For us who remain, Lord, give us strength. Teach us how to mourn with hope, to remember without despair, and to live faithfully until our own journey ends. May [Name]'s legacy inspire us to live with more kindness, more patience, more grace. Comfort every heart that aches because of [Name]'s demise. Wipe every tear. Remind us that love never dies, and that in You, all things are made new.

Until that day when we meet again, hold [Name] close. Let him/her find peace, rest, and eternal joy in Your house, where there is no more death, no more sorrow, no more pain. In the holy name of Jesus Christ (God), we pray, Amen.

SCRIPTURAL READINGS

Psalm 23 (RSV)

1 The Lord is my shepherd; I shall not want;
2 he makes me lie down in green pastures.
He leads me beside still waters;

3 he restores my soul.
He leads me in paths of righteousness
for his name's sake.

4 Even though I walk through the valley of the shadow of death,
I fear no evil;
for thou art with me;
thy rod and thy staff,
they comfort me.

5 Thou preparest a table before me
in the presence of my enemies;
thou anoints my head with oil,
my cup overflows.

6 Surely goodness and mercy shall follow me
all the days of my life;
and I shall dwell in the house of the Lord
forever.
(This psalm is often read at funerals or in times of sorrow and remembrance, offering deep comfort, hope, and assurance of God's eternal care.)

John 14:1–3 (RSV): "Let not your hearts be troubled; believe in God, believe also in me. In my Father's house are many rooms; if it were not so, would I have told you that I go to prepare a place for you? And when I go and prepare a place for you, I will come again and will take you to myself, that where I am you may be also." *(These words of Jesus offer hope and assurance of eternal life.)*

Romans 8:38–39 (RSV): "For I am sure that neither death, nor life, nor angels, nor principalities, nor things present, nor things to come, nor powers, nor height, nor depth, nor anything else in all creation, will be able to separate us from the love of God in Christ Jesus our Lord." *(This passage emphasizes the unbreakable bond of God's love.)*

2 Corinthians 4:16–18 (RSV): "So we do not lose heart. Though our outer nature is wasting away, our inner nature is being renewed every day. For this slight momentary affliction is preparing for us an eternal weight of glory beyond all comparison, because we look not to the things that are seen but to the things that are unseen; for the things that are seen are transient, but the things that are unseen are eternal." *(This reading helps shift focus to the eternal hope promised in Christ.)*

Revelation 21:4 (RSV): "He will wipe away every tear from their eyes, and death shall be no more, neither shall there be mourning nor crying nor pain any more, for the former things have passed away." *(This vision of the new heaven and new earth brings comfort and hope for the life to come.)*

These prayers and readings are tools to create a sacred space where God's presence is deeply felt, offering comfort and hope to the dying and their loved ones.

PRACTICAL REMINDERS

- **Personalization:** Tailor prayers and rituals to the specific beliefs, preferences, and spiritual needs of the individual and their family.
- **Cultural Sensitivity:** Be mindful of cultural traditions and practices that may influence end-of-life care.
- **Presence Over Perfection:** The sincerity of the caregiver's presence matters more than the exact words or actions. Be present, listen, and allow the Spirit to guide the moment.

Appendix 2

Reflective and Discussion Questions

Engaging in meaningful dialogue about end-of-life care, grief, and pastoral support can help individuals, groups, and caregivers reflect, learn, and grow. Below are discussion questions tailored to encourage thoughtful conversations and foster personal and collective insight.

FOR CAREGIVERS SUPPORTING THE DYING

1. **Reflecting on Caregiving**
   - What are some of the emotional challenges you have faced while caring for someone at the end of life?
   - How do you balance providing physical care with offering emotional and spiritual support?
   - In what ways can caregiving be both a burden and a blessing?
2. **Ethical and Spiritual Considerations**
   - How do you approach decisions when a loved one's wishes conflict with medical advice or your personal beliefs?
   - How do faith or spiritual beliefs guide your approach to end-of-life care?
   - What role does forgiveness or reconciliation play in your caregiving relationships?

3. **Coping with Stress and Burnout**

    - How do you manage the emotional toll of caregiving?
    - What self-care practices have you found effective in maintaining your wellbeing?
    - How can communities of faith or support networks better assist caregivers?

FOR GROUPS EXPLORING DEATH AND DYING

1. **Understanding Personal Perspectives**

    - How do your cultural or spiritual beliefs shape your understanding of death and dying?
    - What fears or uncertainties do you have about death, your own or that of a loved one?
    - How do you think society as a whole approaches death? What could be improved?

2. **Navigating Grief and Loss**

    - How do you personally process grief, and what has helped you most during times of loss?
    - What role can community or group support play in helping individuals navigate grief?
    - How do you think anticipatory grief differs from grief after a loss?

3. **Hope and Legacy**

    - What gives you hope in the face of mortality?
    - How can we honor the legacy of those we have lost in meaningful ways?
    - What would you want others to remember or celebrate about your own life?

FOR FAMILIES FACING END-OF-LIFE DECISIONS

1. **Communicating as a Family**
    - How can families create safe spaces to discuss end-of-life wishes openly and honestly?
    - What are some of the challenges of maintaining unity in the family during such difficult times?
    - How can cultural differences or generational gaps impact these conversations?

2. **Making Decisions Together**
    - How do you ensure that a loved one's wishes are respected, even when emotions run high?
    - What factors (e.g., faith, medical advice, quality of life) should guide end-of-life decisions?
    - How do you navigate differences in opinion among family members about care options?

3. **Supporting Each Other**
    - How can family members better support one another emotionally during caregiving and bereavement?
    - What rituals or practices have brought comfort to your family during times of loss?
    - How can you ensure that everyone in the family feels heard and valued during this journey?

FOR GRIEF AND BEREAVEMENT GROUPS

1. **Processing Grief Together**
    - What are some common misconceptions about grief that you have encountered?
    - How does sharing your grief with others in a group setting help (or challenge) your healing process?

- What are some specific ways you can support someone who is struggling with complicated grief?

2. **Spiritual Reflections on Loss**

   - How has your relationship with God or your faith been impacted by your experience of loss?
   - What Scripture passages, prayers, or spiritual practices have brought you comfort?
   - How can faith communities better support those experiencing prolonged or complicated grief?

3. **Looking Toward Hope**

   - How do you define resilience in the context of grief?
   - What signs of hope or healing have you experienced in your grief journey?
   - How can grief shape your outlook on life, relationships, and your purpose?

These reflective and discussion questions provide opportunities for deep reflection, shared understanding, and practical action, fostering a compassionate approach to the challenges of caregiving, grief, and end-of-life care.

Bibliography

American Psychological Association. “Mindfulness Meditation: A Research-Proven Way to Reduce Stress.” October 30, 2019. https://www.apa.org/topics/mindfulness/meditation.

Baker, Edward L. “Self-Care and Mental Health: An Overview.” *Journal of Mental Health* 12 (2003) 145–52.

Ballentine, Jennifer Moore. *End-of-Life Ethics: Communication with Patients and Families.* Washington, DC: Hospice Foundation of America, 2025.

Beauchamp, Tom L., and James F. Childress. *Principles of Biomedical Ethics.* 8th ed. New York: Oxford University Press, 2019.

Bernacki, Rebecca E., and Susan D. Block. “Communication About Serious Illness Care Goals: A Review and Synthesis of Best Practices.” *JAMA Internal Medicine* 174 (2014) 1994–2003. https://doi.org/10.1001/jamainternmed.2014.5271.

Bonanno, George A. *The Other Side of Sadness: What the New Science of Bereavement Tells Us About Life After Loss.* New York: Basic, 2009.

Bonhoeffer, Dietrich. *Letters and Papers from Prison.* Edited by Eberhard Bethge. New York: Touchstone, 1997.

Boss, Pauline. *Ambiguous Loss: Learning to Live with Unresolved Grief.* Cambridge, MA: Harvard University Press, 1999.

Brown, Brené. *The Power of Vulnerability: Teachings of Authenticity, Connection, and Courage.* Louisville, CO: Sounds True, 2012.

Brown, Joseph Epes. *The Sacred Pipe: Black Elk's Account of the Seven Rites of the Oglala Sioux.* Norman: University of Oklahoma Press, 1953.

Brueggemann, Walter. *The Message of the Psalms: A Theological Commentary.* Minneapolis: Augsburg, 1984.

Byock, Ira. *The Four Things That Matter Most: A Book About Living.* New York: Atria, 2004.

———. *Dying Well: Peace and Possibilities at the End of Life.* New York: Riverhead, 1997.

Byrne-Martelli, Sarah. *Memory Eternal: Living with Grief as Orthodox Christians.* Yonkers, NY: St. Vladimir's Seminary, 2023.

Callahan, Daniel. *The Troubled Dream of Life: Living with Mortality.* Washington, DC: Georgetown University Press, 2000.

Callanan, Maggie, and Patricia Kelley. *Final Gifts: Understanding the Special Awareness, Needs, and Communications of the Dying.* New York: Bantam, 1992.

Castro-Figueroa, Eida. "A Biopsychosocial Approach to Grief, Depression, and the Role of Emotional Regulation." *Behavioral Sciences* 11 (2021) 110. https://doi.org/10.3390/bs11080110.

Catechism of the Catholic Church. 2nd ed. Vatican City: Libreria Editrice Vaticana, 1997.

Chochinov, Harvey Max. *Dignity Therapy: Final Words for Final Days*. New York: Oxford University Press, 2012.

Clark, Peter A. *The Ethics of End-of-Life Care: A Case-Based Guide*. Baltimore: Johns Hopkins University Press, 2011.

Craig, William Lane. *Reasonable Faith: Christian Truth and Apologetics*. Wheaton, IL: Crossway, 1994.

Cutis, Randall J., et al. "Intervention to Promote Communication About Goals of Care for Hospitalized Patients With Serious Illness: A Randomized Clinical Trial." *JAMA* 329 (2023) 2028–37. https://doi.org/10.1001/jama.2023.8812.

Damien, Keown. *Buddhism: A Very Short Introduction*. Oxford: Oxford University Press, 2005.

Daniels, Norman. *Just Health: Meeting Health Needs Fairly*. Cambridge: Cambridge University Press, 2008.

Davis, Daphne A., and Jeffrey A. Hayes. "What Are the Benefits of Mindfulness?" *American Psychological Association* 43 (2012) 64. https://www.apa.org/monitor/2012/07-08/ce-corner.

Doka, Kenneth J., and Amy S. Tucci, eds. *Living with Grief: Resilience in the Face of Loss*. Washington, DC: Hospice Foundation of America, 2011.

Doniger, Wendy. *The Hindus: An Alternative History*. New York: Penguin, 2009.

Dorff, Elliot N. *Matters of Life and Death: A Jewish Approach to Modern Medical Ethics*. Philadelphia: Jewish Society, 2003.

Enright, Robert D. *The Forgiving Life: A Pathway to Overcoming Resentment and Creating a Legacy of Love*. Washington, DC: American Psychological Association, 2012.

Ferrell, Betty, and Nessa Coyle. *Oxford Textbook of Palliative Nursing*. 5th ed. New York: Oxford University Press, 2019.

Figley, Charles R. *Compassion Fatigue: Coping with Secondary Traumatic Stress Disorder in Those Who Treat the Traumatized*. New York: Brunner, 2002.

Finnis, John. *Natural Law and Natural Rights*. Oxford: Clarendon, 1980.

Flood, Gavin. *An Introduction to Hinduism*. Cambridge: Cambridge University Press, 1996.

Fretheim, Terence E. *The Suffering of God: An Old Testament Perspective*. Philadelphia: Fortress, 1984.

Gabel, Susan S. *Finding Meaning in Suffering: A Framework for Coping with Terminal Illness*. New York: Oxford University Press, 2015.

Garten, Lars, et al. "Palliative Care and Grief Counseling in Peri- and Neonatology: Recommendations from the German PaluTiN Group." *Frontiers in Pediatrics* 8 (2020) 67. https://doi.org/10.3389/fped.2020.00067.

Gatrad, A. R., and Aziz Sheikh. "Palliative Care for Muslims and Issues Before Death." *International Journal of Palliative Nursing* 8 (2002) 526–31. https://doi.org/10.12968/ijpn.2002.8.11.1089.

Gawande, Atul. *Being Mortal: Medicine and What Matters in the End*. New York: Metropolitan, 2014.

Gillman, Neil. *The Death of Death: Resurrection and Immortality in Jewish Thought*. Woodstock, VT: Jewish Lights, 2000.

Gutiérrez, Gustavo. *On Job: God-Talk and the Suffering of the Innocent*. Translated by Matthew J. O'Connell. Maryknoll, NY: Orbis, 1987.

Halbfass, Wilhelm. *India and Europe: An Essay in Understanding*. Albany: State University of New York, 1988.

Halifax, Joan. *Being with Dying: Cultivating Compassion and Fearlessness in the Presence of Death*. Boston: Shambhala, 2008.

Harvey, Graham. *Animism: Respecting the Living World*. New York: Columbia University Press, 2006.

Harvey, Peter. *An Introduction to Buddhism: Teachings, History, and Practices*. Cambridge: Cambridge University Press, 1990.

Hilberdink, Charlotte E., et al. "Bereavement Issues and Prolonged Grief Disorder: A Global Perspective." *Cambridge Prisms: Global Mental Health* 10 (2023) 1–11.

Hospice Foundation of America. "End-of-Life- Ethics: Communication with Patients and Families." https://hospicefoundation.org/hfa-product/end-of-life-ethics-communication-with-patients-and-families-2/.

———. "Managing Conflict, Finding Meaning." https://hospicefoundation.org/hfa-product/managing-conflict-finding-meaning.

Jacobs, Louis. *The Jewish Religion: A Companion*. Oxford: Oxford University Press, 1995.

Klass, Dennis, et al. *Continuing Bonds: New Understandings of Grief*. Philadelphia: Taylor & Francis, 1996.

Klostermaier, Klaus. K. *A Survey of Hinduism*. Albany: State University of New York Press, 2007.

Koenig, Harold G. *Spirituality in Patient Care: Why, How, When, and What*. Philadelphia: Templeton, 2013.

Kübler-Ross, Elisabeth. *On Death and Dying*. New York: Scribner, 1969.

———. *The Wheel of Life: A Memoir of Living and Dying*. New York: Scribner, 1997.

Kübler-Ross, Elisabeth, and David Kessler. *On Grief and Grieving: Finding the Meaning of Grief Through the Five Stages of Loss*. New York: Scribner, 2005.

Larson-Miller, Lizette. *The Sacrament of the Anointing of the Sick*. Collegeville, MN: Liturgical, 2005.

Liese, Bruce S., and Aaron L. Beck. *Cognitive Therapy of Substance Abuse*. New York: Guilford, 1997.

Lydon-Lam, J. "Models of Spirituality and Consideration of Spiritual Assessment." *International Journal of Childbirth Education* 27 (2012) 18–22.

Margulis, Lynn, and Dorion Sagan. *What Is Life?* Berkley: University of California Press, 1997.

Meier, Diane E. "Family Meetings: A How-To Guide." *Journal of Palliative Medicine* 5 (2002). https://www.liebertpub.com/jpm/.

Meilaender, Gilbert. *Bioethics: A Primer for Christians*. 3rd ed. Grand Rapids: Eerdmans, 2013.

Meyendorff, Paul. *The Anointing of the Sick*. Crestwood, NY: St. Vladimir's Seminary, 2009.

Moitinho, Elias. "Understanding Stress and Burnout in Ministry—Part 1." Liberty University, 2017. Video. https://canvas.liberty.edu/courses/115964/pages/watch-understanding-stress-and-burnout-in-ministry-part-1?module_item_id=17074548.

Moitinho, Elias, and Denise Moitinho. *Dream Home: How to Create an Intimate Christian Marriage*. Dubuque, IA: Kendall, 2020.

Moltmann, Jürgen. *The Crucified God: The Cross of Christ as the Foundation and Criticism of Christian Theology*. Translated by R. A. Wilson and John Bowden. New York: Harper & Row, 1974.

———. *The Theology of Hope: On the Ground and the Implications of a Christian Eschatology*. Translated by James W. Leitch. Minneapolis: Fortress, 1993.

Mura, Gioia, and Mauro Giovanni Carta. "Physical Activity in Depressed Elderly: A Systematic Review." *Clinical Practice and Epidemiology in Mental Health* 10 (2013). https://doi.org/10.2174/1745017901309010125.

Nacak, Ulviye Aydan, and Yasemin Erden. "End-of-Life Care and Nurse's Roles." *The Eurasian Journal of Medicine* 54 (2022) S141–S144. https://doi.org/10.5152/eurasianjmed.2022.22324.

Nasr, Seyyed Hossein. *The Heart of Islam: Enduring Values for Humanity*. San Fransisco: HarperOne, 2002.

Neimeyer, Robert A. *Meaning Reconstruction and the Experience of Loss*. Washington, DC: American Psychological Association, 2001.

Neimeyer, Robert A., et al. *Grief and Bereavement in Contemporary Society: Bridging Research and Practice*. New York: Routledge, 2011.

Nouwen, Henri J. M. *The Wounded Healer: Ministry in Contemporary Society*. New York: Image, 1979.

Olivelle, Patrick. *The* Āśrama *System: The History and Hermeneutics of a Religious Institution*. Oxford: Oxford University Press, 1993.

Orem, Dorothea E. *Nursing: Concepts of Practice*. 4th ed. St. Louis: Mosby, 1991.

Oxford Academic (Oxford University Press). "The Necessity of Self-Care." YouTube, September 28, 2017. Video. www.youtube.com/watch?v=jvENAkUo9YQ.

Park, Crystal L. "Religious and Spiritual Belief." In *Handbook of the Psychology of Religion and Spirituality*, edited by Raymond F. Paloutzian and Crystal L. Park, Guilford, 2013.

Puchalski, Christina, et al. "Improving the Quality of Spiritual Care as a Dimension of Palliative Care: The Report of the Consensus Conference." *Journal of Palliative Medicine* 12 (2009) 885–904. https://doi.org/10.1089/jpm.2009.0142.

———. *Making Health Care Whole: Integrating Spirituality into Patient Care*. West Conshohocken, PA: Templeton, 2010.

Pychyl, Timothy A. *The Psychology of Self-Care: Why It Matters and How to Practice It*. New York: Insight, 2023.

Quill, Timothy E. *Physician-Assisted Dying: The Case for Palliative Care and Patient Choice*. Baltimore: Johns Hopkins University Press, 2004.

Qutb, Sayyid. *In the Shade of the Qur'an: Volume 5 (Surah al-An'ām)*. Translated and edited by Adil Salahi. Leicestershire, UK: Islamic Foundation, 2007.

Rah, Soong-Chan. *Prophetic Lament: A Call for Justice in Troubled Times*. Downers Grove, IL: InterVarsity, 2015.

Rando, Therese A. *Anticipatory Grief and the Family System*. New York: Guilford, 1986.

Ratcliffe, Matthew, et al. "On the Appropriateness of Grief to Its Object." *Journal of the American Philosophical Association* 9 (2023) 318–34. https://doi.org/10.1017/apa.2021.55.

Remen, Rachel Naomi. *My Grandfather's Blessings: Stories of Strength, Refuge, and Belonging*. New York: Riverhead, 2000.

Roberts, Stephen B., ed. *Professional Spiritual and Pastoral Care: A Practical Clergy and Chaplain's Handbook*. Woodstock, VT: Skylight Paths, 2011.

Rosenblatt, Paul C. *Grief: The Social Context of Private Feelings*. New York: Routledge, 2016.

Ryan, Robin. *God and the Mystery of Human Suffering: A Theological Conversation Across the Ages*. New York/Mahwah, NJ: Paulist, 2011.

Sachedina, Abdulaziz. *Islamic Biomedical Ethics: Principles and Application*. New York: Oxford University Press, 2009.

Scalise, Eric. *When Helping You Is Hurting Me: Compassion Fatigue and Making a Commitment to Balanced Self-Care*. N.p.: N.p., 2020. https://share.nned.net/wp-content/uploads/2020/07/Stress_Burnout.pdf.

Shear, M. Katherine. "Complicated Grief." *New England Journal of Medicine* 372 (2015) 153–60. https://doi.org/10.1056/NEJMcp1315618.

Shear, M. Katherine, et al. *Grief and Bereavement in Contemporary Society: Bridging Research and Practice*. New York: Routledge, 2011.

Simon, Naomi M., et al. "Complicated Grief: A Disorder That Impedes Healing After Loss." *American Journal of Psychiatry* 172 (2015) 617–23.

———. "The Diagnosis and Treatment of Complicated Grief: A Review." *JAMA* 312 (2014) 736–47.

Singh, Kathleen Dowling. *The Grace in Dying: A Message of Hope, Comfort and Spiritual Transformation*. San Francisco: HarperOne, 1998.

Smith, John, and Anika Choudhury. *Mental Hygiene: Foundations for Psychological Resilience*. Chicago: MindWell, 2022.

Smedes, Lewis B. *Forgive and Forget: Healing the Hurts We Don't Deserve*. New York: HarperOne, 1984.

Somerville, Margaret A. *Death Talk: The Case Against Euthanasia and Physician-Assisted Suicide*. Montreal: McGill-Queen's University Press, 2001.

Stroebe, Margaret, et al. *Handbook of Bereavement Research and Practice: Advances in Theory and Intervention*. Washington, DC: American Psychological Association, 2008.

Sulmasy, Daniel. "Spiritual Issues in the Care of Dying Patients: '. . . It's Okay Between Me and God.'" *JAMA* 287 (2002) 1385–92. https://doi.org/10.1001/jama.296.11.1385.

Tennent, Timothy C. *Invitation to World Missions: A Trinitarian Theology of the Church's Mission*. Grand Rapids: Kregel Academic, 2020.

Thompson, Becky L., and Robert A. Neimeyer. "Creative Expression and Grief: Testing the Meaning-Making Model." *Death Studies* 38 (2014) 655–67.

Tutu, Desmond, and Mpho Andrea Tutu. *The Book of Forgiving: The Fourfold Path for Healing Ourselves and Our World*. New York: HarperOne, 2014.

United States Conference of Catholic Bishops. *Pastoral Care of the Sick: Rites of Anointing and Viaticum*. Washington, DC: USCCB, 1983.

Volf, Miroslav. *Exclusion and Embrace: A Theological Exploration of Identity, Otherness, and Reconciliation*. Nashville: Abingdon, 2019.

Walter, Tony. *The Revival of Death*. London: Routledge, 1994.

Ward, Keith. *Christian Ethics: A Very Short Introduction*. Oxford University Press, 2021.

Watch Tower Bible and Tract Society of Pennsylvania. *What Does the Bible Really Teach?* Brooklyn, NY: Watchtower Bible and Tract Society, 2005.

Wiesel, Elie. *Night*. Translated by Marion Wiesel. New York: Hill and Wang, 2006.

Williams, Rowan. *The Sign and the Sacrifice: The Meaning of the Cross and Resurrection*. Louisville: Westminster John Knox, 2017.

Wilson, James M. "Resource Allocation at the End of Life: Ethical Considerations." *Journal of Palliative Medicine* 21 (2018).

Wityk, T. L. "Burnout and the Ethics of Self-Care for Therapists." *Alberta Counsellor* 28 (2003) 4–11.

Wolterstorff, Nicholas. *Lament for a Son*. Grand Rapids: Eerdmans, 1987.

Worden, J. William. *Grief Counseling and Grief Therapy: A Handbook for the Mental Health Practitioner*. 4th ed. New York: Springer, 2009.

Worthington, Everett L. Jr. *Forgiving and Reconciling: Bridges to Wholeness and Hope*. Downers Grove, IL: InterVarsity, 2003.

Wright, N. T. *The Resurrection of the Son of God*. Fortress, 2003.

———. *Surprised by Hope: Rethinking Heaven, the Resurrection, and the Mission of the Church*. New York: HarperOne, 2008.

Zylla, Phil C. *The Roots of Sorrow: A Pastoral Theology of Suffering*. Waco, TX: Baylor University Press, 2012.

Index

acceptance
  death as transition, 47
  and forgiveness, 53
  fostering meaning and, 131
  and grief, 23, 26
  and letting go, 48–49
  practical ways of saying goodbye, 115
  sanctity of life, 75
  See also anger; bargaining; denial; depression; mindfulness
active listening. *See* presence and listening
Adam and Eve, 6, 7–8, 16
advance care planning, 78
African traditions, 36
after-death support, 43, 124–28, 133. *See also* end-of-life (EOL) care
afterlife, 5–6, 9–13, 27, 32, 37, 47, 50–51. *See also* eternal life
"Amazing Grace" (hymn), 163–64
American Psychological Association (APA), 30
anger, 23, 25
Anointing of the Sick. *See* Sacrament of the Sick
anticipatory grief
  acknowledgment and validation, 107–8
  emotional care, 109
  helping families navigate, 107–9
  information and education, 108
  living wakes or celebration of life, 110
  opportunities for connection, 108
autonomy, 68, 70, 77, 78–79

Ballentine, Jennifer Moore, 41
bargaining, 23, 25
Beauchamp, Tom L., 68, 71, 73, 77, 78, 91
Beck, Aaron L., 29
beneficence, 68, 70, 71, 74, 78. *See also* autonomy
bereavement
  complicated or prolonged grief, 128–31
  ongoing support, 124–28
Bernacki, Rebecca E., 37–38
Bible
  biblical lament and the human cry, 87–88
  biblical perspectives on dust and eternity, 15–18
Block, Susan D., 37–38
Bonhoeffer, Dietrich, 85, 86
Brown, Brené, 105
Brueggemann, Walter, 88
Buddhism
  caring for the deceased across religions, 36
  death as transition, 5–6
  resurrection and the afterlife, 11–13
  saying goodbye, 114
  spiritual readiness for death, 47–49
burnout, 80, 103, 109, 137, 139, 145

Byock, Ira, 70, 78–79, 94, 95, 96–97, 112–13
Byrne-Martelli, Sarah, 92–93

Carta, Mauro Giovanni, 31
Catechism of the Catholic Church, 59
Catholicism
- caring for the deceased across religions, 34
- sanctity of life, 69
- saying goodbye, 111

Childress, James F., 68, 71, 73, 77, 78, 91
Choudhury, Anika, 138
Christianity
- afterlife, hope for, 50
- biblical perspectives on dust and eternity, 15–18
- death and redemption, 8–9
- death as transition, 6–7, 47
- end-of-life dilemmas, 68–69
- eschatological hope, role of, 154–56
- God's presence, faith and trust in, 156–60
- and hope, 151–53
- hope and resurrection in pastoral theology, 18–21
- legacy, 49
- origin of death, 7–8
- pastoral care and comfort, 119
- resurrection and the afterlife, 10
- Sacrament of the Sick, 59–64
- sanctity of life, 75
- saying goodbye, 113
- spiritual readiness for death, 48
- and suffering, 86
- suffering and redemptive meaning, 90–93
- theological reflection on life and death, 55–59

cognitive behavioral therapy (CBT), 129–30
cognitive function, 31, 144
cognitive reframing, 120
collaboration. *See* coordination of care; holistic approach to grief care
comfort, 57, 113, 154–55, 165
communication, 37–44
community support. *See* spiritual and community support
complicated grief treatment (CGT), 130
complicated or prolonged grief, 118, 128–31
- compassion, approaching with, 129
- meaning and acceptance, fostering, 131
- spiritual and community support, 130–31
- therapeutic interventions, 129–30
- understanding, 128–29

Continuing Bonds Theory, 26
coordination of care, 40, 42, 103–4, 120
coping mechanisms, 24, 26, 29–32, 80, 118, 120, 130, 145

Daniels, Norman, 74
death and dying
- biblical perspectives on dust and eternity, 15–18
- caring for the deceased across religions, 34–37
- cultural and societal attitudes toward, 32–33, 42
- dignity and autonomy, honoring one's, 78–79
- discussion questions, 171–74
- emotional needs, 42, 94–95
- eschatological hope, role of, 154–56
- God as a compassionate witness, 89–90
- God's presence, faith and trust in, 156–60
- holistic self-care, 143–45
- and hope, 151–53
- legal and ethical considerations, 78
- not the final word, 164–66
- origin of, 7–8
- palliative sedation, 72–73
- personal implications, 13–14
- practical implications, 13–15
- presence, art of, 93–94
- and redemption, 8–9
- rituals, 33–34, 96–97
- saying goodbye, 96–97
- self-care for companions, 139–43

spiritual and emotional process of dying, 27–28
spiritual beliefs after, 33–34
spiritual needs, 95–96
stages of grief, 23–24, 25–26
suffering and redemptive meaning, 90–93
theology of, 3–21
See also spiritual readiness for death; theological reflection on life and death
denial, 23, 25, 37, 42, 43, 128
depression, 23, 25–26
dharma, 49–50
dignity, 78–79
Doniger, Wendy, 12
do-not-resuscitate (DNR), 78
double effect, 69, 71, 73
Dual Process Model of Coping, 26

Eastern Orthodoxy, 35, 60
education and preparation, 51, 108
emotional landscape, 103–7
communication and unity, fostering, 104–5
creative expression, 32
dying process, 94–95
emotional process of dying, 27–28
end-of-life (EOL) communication, 42
honoring the legacy of loved ones, 106–7
practical assistance, 103–4
presence, power of, 105
spiritual and psychological support, 105–6
suffering and redemptive meaning, 90–93
emotional self-care, 139–40, 141–42
end-of-life (EOL) care
communication, 37–43
coordination of care, 40, 42, 103–4, 120
death as transition, 46–47
decision-making, 13, 37–38, 40, 41–42, 43, 51, 69, 78, 79–80, 106, 127
eschatological hope, 155
prayers and spiritual readings, 167–70
end-of-life dilemmas, 68–69
autonomy *vs.* beneficence, 70
dignity and autonomy, honoring one's, 78–79
ethics of withholding and withdrawing treatment, 71–72
interconnected process, 79–80
medical interventions and palliative care decisions, 51, 76–79
palliative sedation, 72–73
resource allocation and justice, 73–74
sanctity of life, 75–76
unresolved or complex situations, 80–82
Enright, Robert D., 52, 54
Erden, Yasemin, 46–47
eschatological hope, 153, 154–56
as comfort amid suffering, 154–55
existential and ethical dilemmas, 155
and grief, 155
and resilience, 156
transformative power of, 156
eternal life, 15–16, 17–18, 50, 92, 153, 158, 159–60. *See also* afterlife
ethics. *See* end-of-life dilemmas
euthanasia, 70, 72–73
exercise, 31
Extreme Unction, 60
eye movement desensitization and reprocessing (EMDR) therapy, 130

faith and trust in God's presence through death, 156–60
God's presence, signs of, 159
Jesus' example, 158
mystery, faith in the face of, 159
prayer and worship, role of, 158–59
resurrection, hope in the promise of, 159–60
farewells. *See* saying goodbye
Figley, Charles R., 138
final conversations, 112–13, 114
forgiveness, 52–54

Garten, Lars, 14
generational gaps, 38, 173
Gillman, Neil, 5
God as a compassionate witness, 89–90
God's presence. *See* faith and trust in God's presence through death
grief, 116–35, 166
- anticipatory grief, 107–9
- biblical lament and the human cry, 87–88
- bridging gaps with communication, 37–44
- caring for the deceased across religions, 37
- complicated or prolonged grief, 118, 128–31
- coping mechanisms, 24, 26, 29–32, 80, 118, 120, 130, 145
- cultural and societal attitudes toward, 32–33, 42
- eschatological hope, 155
- finding comfort in, 57
- and guilt, 120–23
- holistic approach to grief care, 119–20
- and hope, 152
- individual dealing with, 124
- long-term effects of, 127
- meaning through action, 43
- personal growth, 44, 135
- psychological impact of, 28–29
- stages of, 23–24, 25–26
- symptoms of, 28, 30–31, 118, 128–30
- *See also* end-of-life (EOL) care

grief counseling, 51, 118–20, 129–30
guilt, 120–23
Gutiérrez, Gustavo, 85, 86

Halbfass, Wilhelm, 50
Halifax, Joan, 97
Harvey, Peter, 12
healing and reconciliation, 27, 54, 156. *See also* acceptance; complicated or prolonged grief; redemption; rituals; Sacrament of the Sick; saying goodbye
healthcare professionals, 104–5
Hinduism
- caring for the deceased across religions, 35–36
- death as transition, 5–6
- legacy of life, 49–50
- resurrection and the afterlife, 11–13
- spiritual readiness for death, 47–48

The Hindus (Doniger), 12
holistic approach to grief care, 119–20
holistic self-care, 143–45
Holy Unction, 60
hope, 151–53, 165–66
- for an afterlife, 50–51
- eschatological hope, 153, 154–56
- and grief, 152
- living with in the present, 153
- meaning-making, nurturing through, 134–35
- renewal in the resurrection of Christ, 152–53
- resurrection, hope in the promise of, 159–60
- and resurrection in pastoral theology, 18–21
- resurrection of Jesus Christ, 151–52
- suffering and redemptive meaning, 91–93

Hospice Foundation of America, 40–43

Igbo, 137
Indigenous traditions, 6, 36, 114
In the Shade of the Qur'an (Qutb), 10
Islam
- caring for the deceased across religions, 35
- death as transition, 5–6, 47
- end-of-life dilemmas, 69
- resurrection and the afterlife, 10
- sanctity of life, 75
- saying goodbye, 113

JAMA, 40
Jehovah's Witnesses, 11
Jesus Christ
- eschatological hope, 154, 155
- eternal life, 17–18
- faith and trust in God's presence through death, 158

God as a compassionate witness, 89
resurrection and hope, 9, 18–21, 91–92, 151–53
Judaism
caring for the deceased across religions, 35
death as transition, 5
end-of-life dilemmas, 69
resurrection and the afterlife, 11
sanctity of life, 75
saying goodbye, 111
justice, 73–74

Keith-Spiegel, Patricia, 137
Keown, Damien, 12
Kessler, David, 24
Klostermaier, Klaus K., 50
Koocher, Gerald P., 137
Kübler-Ross, Elisabeth, 4–5, 23–26, 79, 95, 96, 140

lament, 87–88
Larson-Miller, Lizette, 60
legacy, 49–50, 58–59, 106–7
letting go, 48–49, 54. *See also* Buddhism; forgiveness
Liese, Bruce S., 29
life support, 41, 75
listening. *See* presence and listening

Margulis, Lynn, 5
meaning
fostering meaning acceptance, 131
meaning-making, nurturing through, 134–35
ongoing support to the bereaved, 127
pastoral care and comfort, 119
See also acceptance
medical ethics. *See* autonomy; beneficence
medical interventions and palliative care decisions, 76–79
dignity and autonomy, honoring one's, 78–79
legal and ethical considerations, 78
medical conditions and prognosis, 77
palliative care, 77
See also end-of-life (EOL) care
medications, 72, 130
mental hygiene. *See* self-care and mental hygiene
mental self-care, 139–40, 144
Meyendorff, Paul, 60
mindfulness, 29–30, 138
mindfulness-based stress reduction (MBSR), 30
Moitinho, Denise, 53
Moitinho, Elias, 53, 145
Moltmann, Jürgen, 89, 153, 154
morality, 71–72
mortality. *See* death
Muldary, T. W., 137
Mura, Gioia, 31
mystics, 85, 86

Nacak, Ulviye Aydan, 46–47
Neimeyer, Robert A., 26, 30, 32
Nouwen, Henri J. M., 94, 105

Olivelle, Patrick, 49–50
On Death and Dying (Kübler-Ross), 4–5, 23–26
On Grief and Grieving (Kübler-Ross and Kessler), 24–26
Orem, Dorothea E., 137
Orthodox Christianity. *See* Eastern Orthodoxy

palliative care, 69, 77, 79, 94
palliative sedation, 72–73
pastoral care, 165–66
biblical lament and the human cry, 88
and comfort, 119
end-of-life dilemmas, 69
eschatological hope, 154–56
grief counseling, integrating with, 119–20
pastoral actions, 51–52
Sacrament of the Sick, 61
and silence, 86–87
spiritual and emotional process of dying, 27
spiritual self-care, 140

pastoral care (continued)
suffering and redemptive meaning, 92–93
theological reflection on life and death, 55–56
pastoral theology, role of hope and resurrection in, 18–21
patient wishes, 39–42, 68–69, 71, 73, 74, 77, 78, 79, 80, 104, 106, 111, 114. *See also* end-of-life (EOL) care
physical self-care, 141, 143–44
physician-assisted suicide. *See* euthanasia
practical self-care, 140–41
practical support, 103–4, 127
prayers, 59, 87, 158–59, 167–70
preparatory depression, 25
presence and listening, 27, 51, 81–82, 93–94, 103, 105, 120, 129, 165
professional counseling, 28, 30–31, 103, 106, 109
prolonged exposure therapy (PET), 130
Protestantism, 35
psychological support, 42, 105–6
Puchalski, Christina, 105
Pychyl, Timothy A., 139

Qutb, Sayyid, 10

Rah, Soong-Chan, 88
reactive depression, 25
redemption, 8–9, 90–93
reincarnation, 5–6, 11–12, 34, 50, 119, 134
religious activities, 31–32
resilience
eschatological hope, 156
grieving process, 133
holistic self-care, 144
and hope after loss, 132–35
resource allocation, 73–74
resurrection
and the afterlife, 9–13
eternal life, 7, 17
and hope, 91–92, 151–53, 159–60
and redemption, 8
rituals, 96–97
funeral rites and memorial service, 110
God's presence, 159
honoring the connection to the body, 111
individual dealing with grief, 44, 124
living wakes or celebration of life, 110–11
personal rituals, 110
practices for saying goodbye, 109–15
prayer vigils and blessings, 111
spending quiet time together, 111–12
spiritual and emotional process of dying, 28
spiritual beliefs, 33–34
and traditions, 14
Roberts, Stephen B., 57
Rosenblatt, Paul C., 33

Sacrament of the Sick, 59–64
anointing, rite of, 61
family and friends, role of, 63–64
forgiveness of sins, 61
God's compassion and healing power, 60
key elements of, 62–63
preparation for death, 61
union with Christ's passion, 61
who can receive, 63
Sagan, Dorion, 5
sanctity of life, 75–76
saying goodbye, 96–97
practical ways of, 112–15
rituals and practices for, 109–12
Scalise, Eric, 145
secular contexts, 76, 91, 114
self-care and mental hygiene
balanced life, 144
emotional self-care, 106, 139–40, 141–42, 144
holistic self-care benefits, 143–45
integrating self-care and mental hygiene, 138–39
mental self-care, 139–40, 142, 144
physical self-care, 141, 143–44
practical self-care, 140–41
self-awareness, 144

self-forgiveness, 54
social self-care, 142–43, 144
spiritual self-care, 140, 143, 144
tips for effective self-care, 146
understanding, 137–39
shared decision-making models, 80
Sikhism, 36
silence, 84–87
Smedes, Lewis B., 54
Smith, John, 138
social redemption, 8–9
social self-care, 142–43, 144
societal conventions, 14, 23, 33, 37, 38
spiritual and community support, 44, 51, 92–93, 105–6, 117–20, 124, 130–31. *See also* after-death support; end-of-life (EOL) care; pastoral care
spiritual beliefs, 33–34, 44
spiritual dimension of dying, 27–28, 95–96
spiritual readiness for death, 45–64
acceptance and letting go, 48–49
afterlife, hope for, 50–51
forgiveness and spiritual preparation, 52–54
legacy of life, 49–50
pastoral actions, 51–52
Sacrament of the Sick, 59–64
theological reflection on life and death, 55–59
spiritual self-care, 140, 143, 144
stages of grief, 23–24, 25–26
"Standing on the Promises of God" (hymn), 162–63
stress reduction, 30, 145
suffering
biblical lament and the human cry, 87–88
eschatological hope, 154–55
God as compassionate witness, 89–90
and redemptive meaning, 90–93
and silence, 84–87
support systems, 15, 29, 30, 32, 33. *See also* spiritual and community support

Tasks of Mourning (Worden), 26
Tennent, Timothy C., 18
theological reflection on life and death, 55–59
grief, finding comfort in, 57
hope, preparing for mortality with, 56–57
legacy of faith, encouraging a, 58–59
prayer and Scriptural study, engaging in, 59
purpose, living with, 57–58
sacredness of life, recognizing, 56
therapeutic interventions, 129–30
Thompson, Becky L., 32
touch, 113
Tutu, Desmond and Mpho Andrea, 54

unresolved or complex situations, 27, 94, 114, 120, 139. *See also* complicated or prolonged grief

Volf, Miroslav, 18
vulnerability, 134. *See also* resilience

Ward, Keith, 18
Wicks, Robert J., 144
Wiesel, Elie, 84–85
Williams, Rowan, 86
witness, ministry of, 89–90
Wityk, T. L., 137
Wolterstorff, Nicholas, 85, 86
Worden, J. Williams, 26, 120–21
Worthington, Everett L. Jr., 53, 54
The Wounded Healer (Nouwen), 105
Wright, N. T., 7, 154

www.ingramcontent.com/pod-product-compliance
Lightning Source LLC
LaVergne TN
LVHW050634100826
845148LV00011B/1862

* 9 7 9 8 3 8 5 2 7 1 8 3 2 *